ONLINE MARKETING SECRETS FOR BEGINNERS

DISCOVER THE MOST SUCCESSFUL PRACTICES IN MARKETING AND OUTSMART THE COMPETITION, + 100 MISTAKES BEGINNERS SHOULD AVOID

E.M.P KAILIE

© **Copyright 2021 E.M.P KAILIE - All rights reserved.**

The content contained within this book may not be reproduced, duplicated or transmitted without direct written permission from the author or the publisher.

Under no circumstances will any blame or legal responsibility be held against the publisher, or author, for any damages, reparation, or monetary loss due to the information contained within this book. Either directly or indirectly. You are responsible for your own choices, actions, and results.

Legal Notice:

This book is copyright protected. This book is only for personal use. You cannot amend, distribute, sell, use, quote or paraphrase any part, or the content within this book, without the consent of the author or publisher.

Disclaimer Notice:

Please note the information contained within this document is for educational and entertainment purposes only. All effort has been executed to present accurate, up to date, and reliable, complete information. No warranties of any kind are declared or implied. Readers acknowledge that the author is not engaging in the rendering of legal, financial, medical or professional advice. The content within this book has been derived from various sources. Please consult a licensed professional before attempting any techniques outlined in this book.

By reading this document, the reader agrees that under no circumstances is the author responsible for any losses, direct or indirect, which are incurred as a result of the use of the information contained within this document, including, but not limited to, — errors, omissions, or inaccuracies.

DEDICATION

I dedicate this book to my Parents, my special one, and my three kids, Kim, Abishai, and Abner.

To my Loving Parents, who were my first Teachers, for real the both of them taught me in traditional academic schools. Peace be to his arches; my late Father, Mr. J.S. Paul Kailie, was my very first mentor. As Principle of most of the schools I attended, I salute you, Sir, for the discipline you instilled in me and the hunger you gave me always to learn new things. To my Mother, Madam Anna T. Kailie, who is currently with me as I launch this book, I say thank you, MAMA, for the force you had and always pushed on me as your first child.

To my Special One, Samare Aridi Kailie, thank you for the man and father you made me become. I will always do my best to make you a happy mother.

To my Kids KIM, ABISHAI, and ABNER Kailie, I genuinely love you guys and the challenge you always give me as a dad.

Finally, to all of you reading this book, I love you.

- Emmanuel M.P. Kailie

CONTENTS

Introduction	xiii
1. KNOW THE MARKET AND HOW MARKETING WORK	1
What is marketing?	1
What is the purpose of marketing?	2
The ten types of marketing	3
The essential components of a marketing plan	9
The 4p's of marketing	14
Marketing is not only about selling.	16
Discuss the importance and required focus on the 7P's and the 4 C's	18
The importance of understanding your target audience	21
Building a brand is the most crucial component to successful marketing!	22
2. EMOTIONS ARE EVERYTHING	27
Thus, marketing is all about manipulating emotions.	34
Why do emotions play such a huge role in marketing?	35
Emotional marketing	36
The power and importance of focusing on emotions when marketing	39
The science (and examples) of some powerful and impactful emotional marketing	40

A brief insight into the "dark psychology" of emotional marketing (with emphasis on the positive and productive use of such tactics)	41
The future of marketing is driven by emotion - he who can master the tactics of emotional manipulation will succeed.	44

3. MARKETING THROUGH THE AGES — 47

Where did marketing begin	47
The eras of marketing	50
Now, take a look at the most significant milestones in the evolution of marketing.	52
Change in the past 20 years	55
Change in the past ten years	58
Looking at change year by year in the past decade (emphasizing how rapidly things can change and that one need to be ready for adaptation)	60

4. AVOIDING THE MOST COMMON MISTAKES — 67

1. The market has no clue you exist.	67
2. The market never even heard of you.	68
3. You are not in a position to be known.	69
4. You are not in a position to be heard.	69
5. Your message is not clear, not consistent, and not compelling.	70
6. Your message is not attractive to the market.	70
7. Not enough people hear your message.	71
8. People do not believe you.	71
9. People are not motivated to take action.	72
10. Not Tracking Results	72
11. Ignoring Product Development	72
12. Not Testing Ideas	73
13. Failing to Distinguish Yourself	74
14. Focusing on the Wrong Things	74
15. Trying to Be All Things to All People	75

16. Unclear & Confusing Messaging 76
17. Lack of Authenticity 76
18. Not Participating in the Conversation 77
19. Analysis Paralysis 78
20. Risk Aversion 78
21. Vanity Metrics 79
22. You are not testing. 79
23. Assumption Based Planning 80
24. Trying to be Perfect 80
25. Expecting Immediate Results 80
26. Failure to Launch 81
27. Pivoting Too Often 81
28. Fear of Criticism 82
29. Inability to Prioritize 82
30. Lack of Identity 83
31. No Marketing Budget 83
32. Not Focusing on What Matters 84
33. Forgetting the Human Element 84
34. No Clear Call to Action 84
35. No Urgency 85
36. Trying to Be Like Others 85
37. Not offering discounts 86
38. You are not educating the market. 86
39. No Sense of Urgency 86
40. Avoiding New Media 87
41. Avoiding Social Media 87
42. Not Telling Stories 87
43. Forgetting to Invite Others 88
44. Being Boring 88
45. Not commenting on blogs. 88
46. No lead generation system 89
47. Spamming 89
48. Not retargeting 89

49. Not implementing SEO	90
50. No content strategy	90
51. Not using search engine marketing.	90
52. Not leveraging on video marketing.	91
53. Not nurturing leads	91
54. Turning away guest bloggers	92
55. Poor email marketing	92
56. Not making people feel special.	93
57. No direct mail campaign	93
58. No referral program	94
59. Not doing regular contests & sweepstakes.	94
60. Talking to the wrong people	95
61. Not focusing on retention.	95
62. Doing it all by yourself.	96
63. Not setting marketing goals.	96
64. Not promoting yourself	97
65. Running out of money.	98
66. Not blogging enough	98
67. Not hiring the right people.	99
68. Wrong sample size	100
69. Not taking advantage of paid traffic.	100
70. Not optimizing your site.	101
71. Not managing your pipeline.	102
72. Blindly following the crowd.	102
73. Not doing your research.	102
74. Not taking advantage of word of mouth.	103
75. Not reaching out to influencers.	104
76. Not using testimonials	104
77. Not building relationships	105
78. Taking too much advice	106
79. Not owning your brand.	106
80. Not knowing your numbers.	107
81. Not having a content calendar.	107

82. Not using social media monitoring tools.	108
83. Not using a CRM system.	108
84. Not having a content calendar.	108
85. Not having a set process.	108
86. No auditing process in place	109
87. Searching for a silver bullet	109
88. Not learning from your mistakes.	109
89. Hiding behind your brand	110
90. Unclear target audience	110
91. Not being relevant to the market.	110
92. Not running a controlled experiment.	111
93. Focusing on becoming an expert instead of helping others	111
94. Not reading other people's marketing material.	112
95. Looking for overnight success	112
96. Not going deep enough.	113
97. Focusing on feature instead of benefits	113
98. Trying to be perfect instead of launching.	114
99. Not being open to new ideas.	115
100. Being too attached	115
1. Campaign overspending	116
2. Campaigns not launching on time	117
3. Tracking and Integrations breaking	118
4. Targeting the Wrong audiences	119
5. Broken forms, links, and checkout systems	120
6. Not having a follow-up plan.	122
7. Improper understanding and management of statistics	122
5. WHAT YOU NEED TO KNOW FOR ULTIMATE SUCCESS	124
You've just been shown your blindsides when it comes to marketing.	125
Your Story Matters!	127

Copy is Everything!	129
It's not free...BUT it can be cheap	132
Social Media! Social Media! Social Media!	133
Keeping customers is essential - you can't just "land them" and then move on.	135
Test everything and be open to experimentation - otherwise, you're just running around in the dark.	136
Have Fun!	138
And most importantly - Strategize	138
6. DEVELOPING & APPLYING YOUR STRATEGY	140
Developing your own marketing strategy (and sticking to it - at least long enough to derive usable data) is the most important thing you do for any business.	141
Your strategy will be unique to you and your business.	143
Understand the different methodologies of marketing before getting into building your own strategy	144
Now you know your blind spots!	155
Conclusion	157
References / Resources	159

MASTER MINDSET

FREE GIFT

TO OUR READERS!

DOWNLOAD THE 10 COMMANDMENTS OF A SUCCESSFUL SMART BUSINESS. THE ULTIMATE LIST

www.smartbusinessmindset.com

INTRODUCTION

> "The best marketers are always creating relationships. Relationships with customers, brands and other marketers."
>
> — KURT UHLER, CEO & CO-FOUNDER @ SIDEQIK

Despite putting in a considerable amount of money, time, and research - many marketers fail.

The marketing industry is known for being an extremely challenging and competitive atmosphere. One too many people have tried climbing the ladder of marketing to reach success and have, quite painfully, fallen to their defeat.

But why? What is the reason behind the marketing code so hard to crack?

Well, I'm afraid that there is no short, straightforward answer to this question. So instead, to understand why it's such a struggle for beginners to flourish as marketers, we need to cast an in-depth look into the existing challenges within the marketing industry.

THE BLIND SIDE OF MARKETING

If you have ever attempted to market your product or service to the public and were unsuccessful, then you have probably been a victim of the "Blind Side of Marketing."

This book is written to show you the "Blind Side of Marketing" and help you get past it to succeed in marketing your product or service.

Beginners fail because they did not do their homework.

The beginner does not understand marketing psychology, and they do not know how to market their product or service.

Most beginners think that the only way to market is to start handing out business cards, leaflets, and promotional items to everyone they meet. This is wrong!

There are many other ways to market your product or service that you may not have thought of. This book will show you how to use these methods and become successful.

"If you can't measure it, you can't manage it." Most marketers make the biggest mistake of trying to sell and market to the world when the world is not interested in what they have to offer. So, if you want to make a measurable impact on your marketing, you need to start measuring it.

This is only 1 of the 100 reasons why the world is not seeing your marketing. With all the different strategies, guides, books, and videos on marketing, how can you tell which ones are effective? I was once where you are now.

I spent thousands of dollars on different marketing guides, only to find out that they were not working.

I did not know what to do until I realized that most marketing information is geared towards a specific niche. So, how can you figure out what market you should be in? That is why I wrote this book.

RESEARCH IS AS IMPORTANT AS YOUR STRATEGY

I am a big believer in research. So, before I invest in anything, I like to do my research.

How many times have you been in a meeting with your boss, and they ask you, "Why did this happen?" "Why did we lose the client?" or even, "Why did we lose the account?" It is tough to answer those questions when you are trying to understand the data from a spreadsheet.

The most important thing is that you need to know how to answer these questions before asking. In other words, you need to know what data needs to be collected to be turned into information and knowledge. In addition, once the information and knowledge are collected, it needs to be analyzed for it to be used. However, knowing how to analyze data does not mean that it will work for your company.

In the world of analytics, you need to turn the data into information and knowledge for it to be helpful. You also need to know how to make sense of the data and turn it into something actionable.

This is one of the most significant problems that many companies have. They know how to collect the data, but they do not know how to turn it into information and knowledge. They also do not know how to turn the information and expertise into something actionable. This is a serious problem because you need to know how to make sense of the data and turn it into actionable action.

KNOWING HOW TO COMMUNICATE EFFECTIVELY

Once you have the information and knowledge, you need to be able to communicate it in a way that makes sense. In other words, you need to know how to get the information and knowledge out of your head and into the heads of your audience. This is not as easy as it sounds because some people are visual learners while others are auditory learners. It all depends on what works best for them. In addition, you may have someone who learns by doing, or they may learn by reading. Either way, you will need to find a way to communicate the information and knowledge to work for them.

However, communicating the information and knowledge in a way that makes sense is not enough because you also need to know how to tell stories with data for it to be effective. This means that once you know how to make sense of the data, communicate it in a way that makes sense, and tell stories with data. It will be much easier for people who do not understand analytics or even those who understand analytics but do not use them properly will start using them effectively instead of ignoring them completely.

The digital transformation has changed everything. Not only the markets but also how we communicate and market ourselves in these markets. There are some significant differences between digital marketing and traditional marketing that have to be considered when planning a marketing strategy.

Digital Marketing is always a live process and requires you to be constantly present in the digital space. This includes social media, blogging, press releases, search engine optimization (SEO), pay-per-click (PPC) campaigns, email marketing, mobile marketing, and many more ways of reaching your target audience.

For most companies, this means the need for an integrated online strategy. An online strategy that ensures your brand is visible to your target audience at all times through multiple channels. The biggest challenge for many companies is implementing this integrated online strategy while avoiding some of the most common mistakes companies make when implementing their online system.

The truth is that there are many reasons why companies fail to see results from their online marketing efforts.

One of the greatest fears that the internet marketer faces is not being able to sell products online. As an internet marketer, you are expected to develop a way of selling products or services online and making a profit. This can be very difficult, especially if you are a beginner in this field. To sell products online, you have to be able to make people aware of your business and what it has to offer. This can be very difficult, especially if you do not have any experience in this field.

This is the reason why many internet marketers give up on this venture. This is also the reason why many beginners fail in this field. The secret of selling products online lies in having a strategy that will help you sell products or services. This is what you will learn in this book.

ABOUT THIS BOOK

Unlike the short-form articles you will come across on the same topic, this book has taken its sweet time to come to existence. After years of research, analysis, and case studies, I have unearthed 100 mistakes marketers make that cause them insane detriment.

To make money online, you have to have a marketing strategy that will enable you to sell your products or services. Without such a strategy, you cannot hope to succeed as an internet marketer. This book will help you learn the secret reasons why beginners fail even before they get started in this field.

This book reveals the secrets behind making money online as an internet marketer. These secrets are usually kept by experienced internet marketers who keep them for themselves for obvious reasons. However, with the power of technology and social media, it has become straightforward for anyone to access these secrets and make use of them to make money online. You will learn these secrets in this book and use them for your benefit as an internet marketer.

INTRODUCTION

This book is all about the reasons why your marketing is not working. If you want to be successful in marketing, then you need to read this book.

WHERE THIS BOOK COMES IN

The purpose of this book is not to give you an A-Z account of what marketing is and how you can create the perfect campaign. There are already hundreds of resources out there that will help you do that. Instead, this book is here to answer the ultimate question: why do so many marketers fail?

In 100 Reasons Why, the Market Is Not Seeing Your Marketing, you'll discover:

- The #1 thing you need to do if you want to promote your business successfully — and how to do it
- Powerful insight into the different types of marketing that will make you feel empowered to choose the best one for you and your business
- The essential element in today's marketing world and how it will define the future of business
- How marketing strategies have changed through the years and what you can learn from them
- A comprehensive look at the most common mistakes beginners make and how to avoid them
- 8+ secrets you need to know if you want your business to succeed

- A step-by-step guide to developing and launching your very own marketing strategy

And much more!

Having been someone who has been through the wringer when it comes to marketing, I have tried, tested, and measured hundreds of different marketing strategies. This book will show you the secrets that will help you achieve success in your marketing campaign.

I will also show you some of the mistakes that I made when I was first starting. The mistakes that I made cost me thousands of dollars and took me years to get over.

I have had many mentors in my life, and one of the biggest things they all said was, "Marketing is like a light switch. You turn it on and off." This is the key to your success, and I will show you how to do it in this book.

The statement "learning from others' mistakes" has never been more factual.

My book will also show you the best way to set up your marketing campaign so that you can reach more people, in less time, with less money. This will be done by showing you what I call "the funnel," which is a simple process that will help you achieve success in your marketing campaign.

If you are reading this now, you are one of the lucky ones. You are about to receive the secrets that will help you become successful in your marketing campaign. I have put together a book that will show you what works and what doesn't work.

There's one difference between them and you: they didn't have access to 100 Reasons WHY The MARKET is Not Seeing Your Marketing, but you do!

This book is written in a way that allows you to scan it quickly for specific answers to questions that are commonly asked by small business owners when it comes to marketing. It is also an excellent resource for anyone who needs to teach marketing to others.

This book will help you think outside the box and be creative in your marketing efforts. It will help you understand why it is important to keep marketing even when you are busy running your business. Each reason is clearly stated and easy to understand. Examples are given of existing companies that have made a success of their marketing efforts.

I would recommend this book to anyone who wants to be more creative in their marketing and achieve success in their business or profession.

I will give you 100 reasons why you do not see results in your marketing campaign in the book. It is not your fault. Many things go into marketing that people don't realize or don't know about.

Many things can be done wrong or can be done right, depending on who is doing it. I have been through all of this, and I will share what works and what doesn't work in my book.

By picking up this book, you save yourself thousands of dollars and hundreds of hours of frustration. If you are looking for a shortcut to your success, this is it. I am going to show you how to do it in less time with less money.

If you are looking for a book that will show you how to succeed in your marketing campaign, this is the book for you.

GOING FORWARD

Going into this book, it would serve you well to keep your mind focused on the fact that just because other people made these mistakes, you don't have to! Learn from them, conduct your research and surveys, plan your strategies with a completely aware mindset, and you're good to go.

However, if you fail to do that - if you fail to understand the places where other marketers messed up, then who knows, maybe you'll make it to the next edition of this book...

Want to make sure that doesn't happen? Well then, keep reading!

1

KNOW THE MARKET AND HOW MARKETING WORK

The market is not seeing your marketing. This is because your marketing is weak, boring, or wrong. You will not sell a product or service if the market doesn't understand why they should buy from you. The only thing that can change this is you changing your marketing to a point where the market understands what you have to offer, and when they do understand it, they will buy. This chapter aims to help you understand how the market works (and how it doesn't work). You will learn why the market does not see your marketing or what you are saying in your marketing.

WHAT IS MARKETING?

When we think about marketing, we usually think about advertising. We think about the use of words and graphics to sell a product or service. We think about using colors, shapes, and logos to convey a message to the market. But marketing is not just advertising; marketing is everything that you do to get someone to buy a product or service from you. Marketing is everything you do to get someone interested in what you have to offer. Marketing is everything from your website, sales presentations, offers, and even your interactions with prospects.

Marketing is what creates interest in what you have to offer. The more interest you make in your products and services, the more likely they will buy from you. If people only see one option for getting something done, then they will choose that option every time (even if it's not the best option).

WHAT IS THE PURPOSE OF MARKETING?

The purpose of marketing is to get people to buy your products or services. Marketing can not be about you; and it has to be about them. Marketing is a way for you to educate people about what you have to offer and why they should buy from you (and not someone else).

Marketing is also a way for you to show the market that what you have to offer will help them reach their goals. It's not enough for them to be interested in what you have to offer. The market must believe that what you have to offer will help them reach their goals.

Marketing aims to create an educational conversation with your prospect to understand why your products and services will help them reach their goals. For this conversation or relationship between the market and yourself to succeed, the market must trust you and your business. It takes time and effort on your part (and if you are smart, some money as well). The more time and effort that goes into marketing, the more successful your business will become.

THE TEN TYPES OF MARKETING

1. Content Marketing

Content marketing is the creation of content that will attract people to your product or service. It can be as simple as a blog post, a short article, a video, an e-book, an audio file, or something else too. The idea behind content marketing is to create something that will attract the right people who are interested in what you have to offer.

For example, suppose you're going to sell a weight loss product. In that case, you want to create content that will attract people interested in losing weight. You don't want to start blogging about random topics because you have no idea who is reading your blog. You need to know what your audience wants or needs before you create content for them.

Content marketing is so powerful that it allows you to capture people's attention without using any complicated selling techniques. People will only read your content if they are interested in the topic, and then they will follow up with you if they have questions.

2. Social Media Marketing

Social media marketing uses social media sites like Facebook, Twitter, YouTube, Instagram, Pinterest, Google+, and others to attract people interested in what you have to offer. This type of marketing requires that you create content for your social media profiles that attract people interested in what you have to offer (if there's no interest, then there will be no sales).

Social media marketing is excellent because it allows for videos, images, and text posts to get a lot more attention than traditional text posts on websites like blogs. It also allows you to reach out to people interested in what you have to offer without them having to look for you.

3. Email Marketing

Email marketing sends emails and newsletters to your prospects and customers who have already expressed interest in what you have to offer. You can use an email list, a list of people who already bought from you, or some type of opt-in list to email people about offers or updates that might be interesting to them.

Email marketing is great because it allows for different types of content (images, video, text) that will get more attention than just text on websites or social media profiles. Email marketing is also great because it allows you to contact people directly without having to worry about whether they will want your product or service or not. This type of marketing requires that your previous offers are attractive enough not to turn off those receiving your emails by making them irrelevant or annoying.

For example, if you start giving your email list the same sales pitch you're offering on your website, you will quickly lose them. You have to make sure that your content in all of your marketing channels (offline and online) is relevant and exciting for the people receiving it.

4. Community Marketing

Community marketing is marketing to a group of people who are interested in what you have to offer. This type of marketing can be done by joining or creating a group, an online forum, or even a Facebook group where you can discuss topics related to what you have to offer. It can also be done by commenting on other blogs, YouTube videos, and other social media profiles where people are interested in what you offer.

Community marketing is excellent because it allows for images, videos, and text posts that are more interesting than just text on websites or social media profiles (not to mention easier to create). It's also great because you can interact with people who already know about what you have to offer. They might want more information or an opportunity from you.

5. Search Engine Optimization

Search engine optimization (SEO) aims to get your website or web page to show up on the first page or 10 of Google, Yahoo, Bing, and other search engines when people are searching for related content. Many factors go into SEO, including on-page SEO (title tags, meta descriptions, alt tags, etc.), inbound links from other websites, anchor text from other websites, and social shares.

SEO is great because it allows you to show up on the first page or ten search engines when you have relevant content that will attract the right people. It's also great because it allows you to potentially reach millions of people without even having a website if you use social media profiles like Facebook and Twitter.

6. Public Relations and Press Releases

Public relations is getting coverage about yourself or your business by journalists in newspapers and magazines. Press releases are most often used for something newsworthy, like a new product release or an upcoming event.

Public relations is excellent because it allows you to reach large audiences that you could not achieve independently. Journalists can get an audience that is millions of times larger than what you could get by just posting something on your social media profiles or website.

7. Search Engine Marketing

Search engine marketing (SEM) is online advertising on search engines like Google, Bing, and Yahoo. It's usually done through paid ads (which are called AdWords). SEM aims to get people to click on your ads and then come to your website or web page.

SEM is great because you can get people to click on your ads who would not have come to your website or webpage otherwise. It's also great because it allows you to show up on the first page or ten search engines without having much content or a website.

For example, if you manage to get your ad on the first page or 10 of Google, people will see your ad when searching for related content. Then, if they click on your ad, they will come to your website or webpage.

8. Inbound Marketing

Inbound marketing is the newest and one of the most effective forms of online marketing. Inbound marketing focuses on attracting customers to come to your website, rather than you having to go out and market to them.

Inbound marketing involves using content to attract customers by offering them helpful information. This information can be in the form of blog posts, eBooks, video tutorials, and webinars.

Your goal with inbound marketing is not to sell at first sight but to provide valuable information to make your prospects want more.

Once you start getting traffic to your website, you can begin converting those visitors into leads and eventually customers.

Inbound marketing works exceptionally well for B2B companies with products and services that are more complex and require a longer sales cycle.

As consumers, we're used to being marketed to. We're constantly bombarded with advertisements from the minute we wake up until we go to bed. As a result, we've become immune to all of the marketing messages that we were subjected to every day. This is one reason why inbound marketing is so effective — it breaks through all of this clutter.

9. Referral Marketing

Referral marketing is when a customer refers you to a friend or colleague. Just like inbound marketing, referral marketing relies on the power of content to attract customers.

Instead of providing valuable information, referral marketing involves offering your customers the ability to refer their friends and family for discounts and rewards.

For example, you can offer your customers a discount or free shipping if they refer someone else. You can also offer them rewards such as gift cards or points that can be redeemed for merchandise.

The goal of referral marketing is to attract more customers by rewarding those who already love your business enough to refer it to others.

10. Industry Exhibitions

Industry exhibitions are an excellent way to promote your brand and build your reputation. They're also great for networking with other businesses.

Industry exhibitions come in all shapes and sizes. For instance, you can go to any trade show that happens to be in town, or you can attend a local seminar or conference.

This is particularly useful for B2B companies who want to make a name for themselves.

THE ESSENTIAL COMPONENTS OF A MARKETING PLAN

When it comes to marketing, we are often told about the four essential components: product, price, promotion, and place. Indeed, a business will not succeed without a good product or service. It is also vital to understand that marketing plans are only as good as their strategy and tactics.

However, many of us have been in situations where we have had excellent products and services. However, we were still unable to attract customers because of our inability to market them effectively. This is where the missing link comes into play. Marketing plans are only as good as their strategy and tactics.

Market Research

The first step in a marketing plan is to have an understanding of the market. The market is the group of people or organizations who are potential buyers for your product or service.

If you are selling to businesses, you must start with a company market research report. This report will give you a comprehensive overview of the company and its organization. You can find out about its current problems, goals, and what they are doing to solve them.

You can also find out about how much money the company makes and how it is performing.

Once you have the information from your company's market research report, you can move on to a customer market research report. This is an in-depth study of your target customers or clients. This kind of study will reveal their likes and dislikes, their problems and frustrations. It will tell you what they want most from your product or service and how much they are willing to pay for it.

Positioning

Once you have an understanding of the market, you are ready to develop your marketing plan.

There is more to a marketing plan than just having a product or service. Whether your product or service is good or bad, it will not sell unless you know how to position it in the market.

You can position your products and services in many ways:

Quality: The quality of your products and services can be perceived as superior, inferior, acceptable, or somewhere in between. This perception will decide the price of your product.

Features: Some products have features that make them more appealing, desirable, or necessary than similar products. Sometimes the parts are not actual, but they become perceived as necessary because of some intangible quality.

Benefits: The benefits of a product or service determine what the market will gain from using it.

Pricing: Pricing is determined by the target market, its perception of quality, features, and benefits.

Promotion: Promotion is the process of letting people know about your product or service through advertising and other forms of communication.

Place: Place refers to where you place your product or service in the market. If you want to sell a product in an expensive shop where much prestige can be gained, you will have to put a high price. If you're going to sell it in a store next door to your competition, you will have to put a low cost.

Competitive Analysis

After you have done your market research, you should know the competition well. You should know who they are, where they are, how much they sell their products or services, and what they can do for your product or service.

You should also consider the competition's strengths and weaknesses. What are some of their characteristics? Are they doing things differently from you? Are they using a different strategy? If so, can you learn from them?

Market Strategy

You should know your customers and what they want from your product or service. You should also know your competition well. These two factors will guide you in developing your marketing strategy.

The strategy you develop will determine how you will market your product or service, how much you will sell it for, what sales plan you will use, and how much money you can expect to make.

Budget

The budget is one of the essential parts of your marketing plan. It will tell you how much money you will spend on marketing and what the returns will be.

It will also indicate what kind of market research you can do and how much money you need to do it.

Metrics

The last part of your marketing plan is the metrics. This will tell you how well your campaign is doing and guide you in making improvements if necessary. Your metrics will answer questions like:

What is your sales performance?

How much did you make?

What were your costs?

What are the problems that you encountered?

Your marketing plan should include both qualitative and quantitative data. The qualitative data provides background information, market research data, marketing strategies, product or service descriptions, and more. The quantitative data include sales performance, costs, and more. Combining these two different types of data will help you make improvements in the future.

THE 4P'S OF MARKETING

When it comes to marketing, we need to know the 4Ps of marketing. We need to know what the market is, how they think, and their needs and wants. We also need to know how to capture their attention, retain it, satisfy them, and position ourselves in the marketplace.

1. The Product:

The product is the first P of marketing, and it is what the market wants. It is how we are going to satisfy their needs and wants. It is what they are looking for when they buy a specific product. The product itself must be an outstanding one that can stand out in the marketplace.

2. The Price:

Price is also an essential part of marketing since it has to do with finance. When we are selling a product, we need to know the price to make it competitive in the marketplace. We need to know if our price is correct or if we need to adjust it to fit with the market price, so we have good sales and good business.

If our price goes too high, then no one will buy our product anymore because everyone can get something similar at a lower price and vice versa if our price is too low then no one will see us as quality products anymore and think that you are offering your products at such a low price just because you don't put much effort or time into them which means people won't buy your products anymore because they think you don't care about what you do or how hard you work for your business anymore.

The price that we put on our products must be reasonable, so people can buy them and see us as an attractive business.

3. The Place:

The place refers to the location of the product. We need to know where our customers are located for us to sell them our products. Since the market is a prominent place, we need to plan on which area we want to focus on in terms of selling our products and what kind of place we want to put our products in. We have to make sure that the place we put our products is not far from where most of our customers or potential customers will be going. They can easily visit us when they need or want something or want information about our product. If we are selling cars, it would be good to set up an office near car dealerships since most of the people who go there will also be interested in buying a new car someday. If you have your own car brand, you can be one of their options when they are ready to buy a new car.

4. The People:

The people part refers to knowing who your target audience is and whom you want your product to sell. The people part also deals with knowing your target demographic to understand better who our customers are. If we are selling cars, it will be good for us to know the ages of the people who buy cars or if they are male or female because they have different needs and wants in a vehicle. These different needs and desires need to be satisfied and satisfied by our product to attract more of their kind, so they will keep coming back for more cars from us.

The 4p's are very important when it comes to marketing because they help us better understand the market that we want to sell our products in and how we need to sell our products to sell well.

MARKETING IS NOT ONLY ABOUT SELLING.

Many business owners fail to understand the importance of Marketing.

Marketing is not just about selling:

It is about positioning the product or service in the marketplace to be accepted and actually purchased. It is about providing an image that the consumer wants to buy into. It is about educating the consumer on the product or service and showing them how it will enhance their lives.

Marketing is also not just a one-time thing:

It is an ongoing process. It does not stop when the consumer buys and takes delivery of the product or service. It does not stop when they start using it. It continues throughout their ownership of the product or service.

This means that Marketing has to be a part of every aspect of your marketing program from the first time you decide to do business with a customer, through every sale, and every day after buying your product or service until they choose to no longer do such a business with you.

Marketing needs to be as much a part of your business as any other aspect of your business practice. You have to put just as much time, money, and effort into marketing as you do with everything else in your company if you will be successful in selling your product or service, which will result in success for your company.

DISCUSS THE IMPORTANCE AND REQUIRED FOCUS ON THE 7P'S AND THE 4 C'S

1. Product

The product is the first P in the 7P's. The product is what you are selling. It is the physical or service that you are offering to your customers. When a customer buys your product, they will benefit from it. For example, a customer buys laptop because they need them for work, school, or entertainment.

2. Placement

It is the second P in the 7P's. Placement involves where you place your product in the market. It applies whether you place your product inside a store, at the cashier's counter or the store entrance, or somewhere else in a mall. Placement also involves how you arrange your display to highlight your product and make it attractive to customers.

3. Promotion

Promotion is the third P in the 7P's. Promotion involves all the marketing activities that let people know about your product, including advertising, email marketing, direct mail, social media, and more. It also includes all of our activities and our website and other content we create — all are done to promote our products and services and attract customers to buy them.

4. Price

Price is the fourth P in the 7P's. Price is the amount of money you charge for your product. It involves the price of your product and even the price you charge for shipping or delivery.

5. People

The fifth P in the 7P's is People. It involves all of the people involved in your marketing efforts, including employees, contractors, and freelancers like graphic designers and web designers. It includes all of your partners, customers, and vendors who help you market your product or service. Every person involved will positively or negatively contribute to your marketing efforts, so it is essential to have great people on board who are committed to helping you succeed in marketing your product or service.

6. Physical Space

Physical space is the sixth P in the 7P's. Physical space involves all of your physical assets, including buildings, offices, factories, and transportation equipment. It also includes all the equipment and tools you need to help you do your marketing work.

7. Process

The process is the seventh P in the 7P's. The process involves all of your processes and procedures for making or delivering your product or service to customers. It includes everything from designing a product to how it is made, packaged, and shipped to customers. It also has how you train employees and other people to produce or sell products or provide services to customers.

1. Customer

The customer is the first C in the 4 C's. The customer is whom you are marketing to. It includes people and businesses who want, needs, or buy your product or service. It also involves people who may not need your product now but maybe a potential customer in the future if you can attract their attention and interest today.

2. Channel

Channel is the second C in the 4 C's. Channel refers to where you market and sell your product or service. It refers to the stores, websites, social media, email marketing campaigns, and other places where you market and sell your products or services to customers.

3. Communication

Communication is the third C in the 4 C's. It refers to how you communicate with customers and potential customers, including through social media, websites, email marketing, and more.

4. Cost

Cost is the fourth C in the 4 C's. Cost refers to how much it costs you to market your product or service or produce it for sale. It includes all of your costs and any fees you charge customers for shipping, delivery, or other services you provide with your product or service.

THE IMPORTANCE OF UNDERSTANDING YOUR TARGET AUDIENCE

The goal of every marketing campaign is to reach the target audience. Many businesses have launched an aggressive campaign but failed to see any results because they didn't know their target audience.

It's vital that you know your target audience as thoroughly as possible because it will enable you to reach them most effectively.

The following are ways to understand your target audience:

- Know their interests, needs, and challenges.
- Understand their demographics.
- Learn the lifestyle of your target audience.
- Know what kind of language your target audience uses.
- Identify the media channels that are used by your target audience.

By knowing all this information about your target audience, you'll be better able to develop a marketing campaign that will reach them effectively.

BUILDING A BRAND IS THE MOST CRUCIAL COMPONENT TO SUCCESSFUL MARKETING!

Building a brand is not about what you do but about who the customer is and what they want. People do **not** buy what you do; they buy why you do it. The reason why is a story, and the story is based on a problem that your customers have. The reason why only becomes clear when you know the market that you are serving.

To know the market, marketers must develop a deep understanding of the market.

When you understand the market, then you can develop a niche story that defines your market and your product or service.

Why it's important:

A brand is a promise. You promise your customers that you will solve a problem. The reason why is the assurance that you make to the customer.

Understanding your market and how marketing work requires an understanding of the customer's needs, wants, and problems:

A good marketing person knows the market and how to market and knows the customer and what they want. They also know how people buy, i.e., through social proof, and how they respond to advertising (what they remember). They also know the basics of marketing: what makes a good offer (value) and understanding why people buy (because it solves their problems). A good marketer knows what price to charge – not too little or too much – priced based on value. They know what makes them different from others in the market and have researched their competitors.

How to do it:

What you do in marketing is based on what you learn about your market. The better you understand your market, the better your product will be.

A good marketer knows that they can't do everything themselves. They know that they need a team to help them create their product and marketing. They know how to choose the right team for their project.

Marketing is not just about creating a product or service, but what you do with it after it's been made:

Marketing is not done in a vacuum; it has to be done within the context of existing products and services in your market – and what other people are doing with theirs. Marketing has to be done with careful consideration of what products already exist (and which of those may already serve the same customer needs as yours) as well as what customers want and are currently buying (what are other companies/people selling). Marketing must fit within the context of all these factors; if it does not, then marketing won't work. Marketing that does not fit into the existing market is doomed to fail – even if it's a great idea. It takes someone who understands these factors and can properly incorporate them into their marketing plan.

Benefits of doing so:

A good marketer knows how to find out what the market needs and wants (through research), and how to do it without spending much money. They know how to create a product or service to meet the customers' needs, wants, and problems. They know which customer groups to target, why they should be targeted, and how best to reach them and get their attention. They know how to create a marketing plan that will work – i.e., one that is good for both the customers and the business, attracting customers at an affordable price for the company (and making it profitable).

The marketer who understands all these things is worth their weight in gold. This is what separates the successful from the unsuccessful in marketing.

If you don't understand your market, you will fail with marketing no matter how much time, money, and effort you put into it. Understanding your market is the first and most important part of marketing.

Highlight some of the most successful brands and how their brand essentially takes care of their marketing for them:

1. Apple: Their brand is all about simplicity, convenience, and ease. It's a brand that focuses on beauty, elegance, and ease of use. Apple products are designed to be easy to use and easy to hold. They have mastered the art of creating a user experience for their customers.

2. Harley Davidson: The Harley Davidson motorcycle is a tough, powerful machine designed for those of us who love speed and danger (and they have great leather jackets). The Harley Davidson brand is very image-based. It has a macho feeling that attracts people who want to feel like they are bad-ass bikers (and are willing to pay much money for it).

3. Starbucks: Starbucks is about premium coffee with luxury design and atmosphere – an experience rather than just a product. It's all about the "coffee shop" experience – not just about coffee, but about relaxation, atmosphere, and community with your friends (not just a place where you get your morning coffee).

4. Microsoft: We all know that Microsoft products are not always the best, but they have created an image of being better than anyone else – even if that's not true. Many people buy into this image – and Microsoft makes much money off of it.

These are some of the most successful brands globally – and they have created an image that efficiently solves their marketing problems for them.

The key is to create a brand that matches your marketing plan (and create a marketing plan that works with your product or service).

2

EMOTIONS ARE EVERYTHING

Let's take a look at human beings and the fact that we are very emotional creatures. We are emotional beings, and we have to realize that emotions are the key to selling. I've heard many people say, "Oh, it's all about logic and facts." But it's not. It's all about emotions.

I'll give you an example. I talked with my wife the other day, and she told me, "I want a new car." She said that she just wanted the car because there is an AWD (All Wheel Drive) option, and it is better in the snow. And I told her that I thought that was very logical.

But then she said to me, "You know what? It's not just because of the safety reasons or better because of the snow; it's because of how it makes me feel when driving up a mountain into Tahoe in January."

She said that there are two reasons she wanted this car – one is logical (safety). One is emotional (feeling of pleasure). And neither one or both together make up for something called emotionality, which is a fancy word for feelings. And emotions make us do things – they make us move in certain ways; they tell us what to do; they tell us how to feel and what to think.

So, when you're selling, the key is to use emotions because they're the key. And if you can get people to do something based on what they feel is correct, then you've got a winner there, and you've got somebody who will buy from you.

The human is a social and emotional being by essence and nature:

So, let's take a look at what this means. We are social beings. This means that we like to be around other people; we want to associate with other people. And that's a good thing because, in order to learn something and find solutions to problems, we have to be around other people.

We need to solve problems together as a tribe or as a group and not as an individual. So, when you're selling something, you're selling it as part of a tribe – it's not just you selling something by yourself; it should be part of the whole package and what makes up the entire package is the tribe or the group of people who work together for mutual benefit and mutual gain – in other words, for profit. Profit is good for the individual and good for the group or business organization.

But we're also emotional beings. This means that when we feel something, we act in a certain way. For example, if we see someone who is in pain, we want to help them. We want to give them relief.

If we see someone who is sad, we want to make them happy. If someone is happy, we want to make them more comfortable. If somebody is angry, we want to calm them down. We're very emotional creatures, and our emotions tell us what to do, and they tell us how to feel; they tell us how we should act.

And so, when you're selling something, you have to use emotional triggers. You have to figure out what the emotions are that are motivating them or inspiring them, or pushing them into doing something. Then you know how to use those emotions, and then you know how to design your marketing message around those emotions so that they can buy from you and lead a more productive life.

We often make our decisions from an emotional point of view:

When we make decisions, we often make them based on our emotions and not based on logic. For example, when I got married to my wife – I don't think it was a logical decision. I didn't say to myself, "Well, let me see what the statistics are about getting married."

I didn't look at the statistics and go through a chart of things. No. It was an emotional decision that I made because I wanted to be with her always. And so, it wasn't a logical decision; it was an emotional decision. And what emotions did I feel? Love, happiness, joy, and pleasure.

When you're selling something to somebody, you have to figure out what their emotions are. And you have to figure out what they feel is right for them and how they think about it. And then, you have to design your marketing message around those emotions.

Even if we think we are logical and rational:

So, when we make decisions, we think that we are logical and rational. But I have to tell you that frequently, we are making our decisions based on emotions and not based on logic.

For example, I was talking with a friend of mine about the stock market one day, and he said to me, "I think I'm going to invest in the stock market." And I said to him, "Why? Why now?" And he said to me, "Oh, look at all the numbers. It's a good time now."

And then he went on a long dissertation about how much money you could make in the stock market right now if you invested directly. But then when I asked him why he wanted to invest in the stock market right now rather than next year or two years from now or five years from now or ten years from now; he couldn't give me an answer except for saying that it was a good time because of all these statistical reasons.

So, when you're selling something – be it financial services or whatever – you have to create a picture of prosperity. You have to create a picture of how this will make someone feel happy and how it will make them feel wealthier.

In other words, we have to create an image or a vision of how this will make someone feel happy and how it will make them feel wealthier. And that's what success is all about: making people happy and making them feel like they are successful in life.

If you can do that, then you have a winner there; you have a winner because if you can make somebody happy, they'll continue to be your customer forever – or as long as they are living. And if you can make somebody more successful, then that's the key right there.

How emotions play a role in our decision-making process

Now, when we're making decisions, we're not analytical and rational. We think that we are, but most of the time, our emotions control what we do and how we feel. Suppose you're a logical person, which I am not. In that case, I'm a very emotional person – then you'll know that when you're making decisions, they're based on emotions.

You make them based on your emotions. Then you think about doing something logical afterward to justify it and rationalize it.

So, if somebody's angry at us or is happy with us or is sad with us or loves us or hates us, our actions will be different.

And so, what this means is that when you're selling something to your customers, the customers who are happy with you will buy from you again and again because they already like what they've got; they enjoy the experience that they've had with you; the results that they've obtained from working with you are beneficial for them; so why not keep doing what they're doing?

?., But those customers who have been unhappy with their experience will leave because their emotions tell them not to come back. So it doesn't matter how good the product is or how good the service is; if the customer doesn't like you, if they don't have a good feeling about you, then they're not going to come back.

And so, this means that in marketing, you have to find ways to make yourself more likable and more lovable, and more trustworthy. And this is something that all of your marketing material has to do with.

And so, when you're creating your marketing messages, your marketing materials need to evoke emotions – it has to have a positive feeling attached to it. It can be happiness – it can be joy; it can be exciting; it can be hope: whatever it is that would be appealing and attractive for the customer or the prospect, then that's what you want your message to do. You want them to feel something when they see your message and when they see what you're doing.

You want them to feel something positive about what you're doing. And once you've done that, they know that they can trust you because if they trust you, they already know what kind of experience they'll get from working with you.

So, just remember these two things: first of all:

Marketing Is For Human Beings

And secondly:

Marketing Is About Emotions

Now that you know this, it's time to create marketing and sales messages that work.

THUS, MARKETING IS ALL ABOUT MANIPULATING EMOTIONS.

Most marketers know marketing is about triggering emotions, but they don't know what to do about it.

They are afraid, even scared of emotions. They are afraid that people will think they are manipulating them if they use emotions in marketing. They're often scared that if they show their true colors instead of hiding behind the corporate façade, people won't trust them anymore. They think that showing emotion might hurt their credibility or make them look weak. They fear that showing their true colors might make people change their opinion about them, and they really don't want people to change their opinion about them.

Well, here's a secret:

People already know you are manipulating them!

They may not know precisely how you are doing it, but they know you are doing it. You might also use it to your advantage instead of hiding the fact that you are playing with their emotions. Manipulating emotion is a good thing. It means that you care enough about people to manipulate their emotions for the betterment of all concerned. This is what love is all about. Love manipulates emotions for the betterment of all concerned. The more you can influence someone's emotions in favor of your product or service, the more that person will feel loved by you. The more likely they will be to do whatever it takes to give you money in exchange for your product or service.

WHY DO EMOTIONS PLAY SUCH A HUGE ROLE IN MARKETING?

Emotions play such a significant role in marketing because emotions are the currency of marketing. All successful marketing campaigns use some form of emotion as their currency. Without the proper emotional appeal, you can't have a successful marketing campaign. Once you know your customer's needs and wants are expressive, you will create the right product or service to meet their needs and wants.

The more emotionally appealing your products or services are to your target market, the more successful you will be at selling them in the future when your products or services meet their needs and want at that time. Therefore, every business owner/salesperson needs to understand this concept to make sure they create and sell emotionally appealing products and services to their customers.

EMOTIONAL MARKETING

The key to marketing success for any business is to make your product or service emotionally appealing to your target market. Emotional marketing is a vital component in the entire marketing mix. Emotionally appealing information or entertainment (product) to your target market (customer) will lead to sales and profits.

The most successful businesses are unfailingly involved with emotionally appealing materials, whether radio, television, magazines, newspapers, direct mail, or any other advertising or media outlet. Therefore, the more emotionally appealing materials you create and use, the more successful you will be at marketing your business.

It's not what you say that's important; it's what your product is saying about itself that counts:

This rule of thumb will help you learn how to create the right products and services for your customers. To make an emotional connection with your customers, you must first understand their needs and wants. Once you know what they want and need from you as a business owner or salesperson, then you can begin creating products and services that meet those needs and wants. No customer will buy from a person they don't like; therefore, every business owner or salesperson needs to be likable.

If you want to be liked, then you need to learn how to listen to your customer. Before customers open up and tell you what they want and need, they must feel comfortable with you. To make them feel comfortable, they need to trust you first. Trust can only come from consistently providing them with the products and services that meet their needs and wants. Once they trust you, then you will have a relationship with them that can lead to a sale in the future when your products or services meet their needs at that time.

To make someone like you, show that person that you care about them by listening to what they have to say. Asking questions about their personal lives, family, friends, business experiences, etc., will let them know that you are interested in them as a person and not just as a prospective customer. This is an essential aspect of emotional marketing because once the customer feels comfortable with and trusts you as a business owner or salesperson, then they will open up emotionally by telling you what their needs are in their business or personal life at the time of your conversation with them. Once you have accomplished this, you will have a customer for life! Once this happens, you have to find out how your product or service meets their needs.

The key to emotional marketing is to find out what your customer's needs are and then find out how your product or service meets those needs. This means that when you're meeting a person for the first time, it is imperative that you listen to what they have to say, whether it is personal or professional. The more they talk, the more they will open up emotionally and tell you about their business and personal lives. The more they tell you about their lives, the more comfortable they will feel around you. The more comfortable they feel around you, the more likely they will buy from you in the future when your products or services meet their needs and want at that time.

As a business owner, salesperson, marketer, etc., your goal is to make them like you as a person, find out what their needs are in business or personal life, and then find out how your products or services meet those needs. Once this happens, all you have to do is say "thank you" for telling me about your business/personal life and telling them how your products or services meet those needs. This is where the sale comes into play. You will have a customer for life and the potential to make much money from that customer on a repeated basis.

The more you can make someone emotionally attached to your product or service, the more successful you will be at selling it to them in the future. The key to being successful is to make people feel comfortable around you and trust you first, then listen to what they have to say about their business/personal life, then ask questions about what their needs are in their business/personal life at that time, and finally show them how your products or services meet those needs. It's not what you say, but it's what your product or service is saying about itself that counts in emotional marketing.

THE POWER AND IMPORTANCE OF FOCUSING ON EMOTIONS WHEN MARKETING

The power and importance of focusing on emotions when marketing is crucial because emotions enable you to have a successful marketing campaign. Your target market's emotions are the currency or token that allows you to enter their minds, hearts, and souls and gain their trust. When you gain your customers' trust, then they will be willing to buy from you over anyone else.

Without focusing on your target market's emotions, it won't matter how good of a salesperson you are because you won't be able to gain your customers' trust. That is why it is so important for all business owners/salespeople to understand this most important marketing concept.

Suppose your business does not focus on selling emotionally appealing products or services to your target market. In that case, you could be missing out on some very profitable opportunities in the future. On the other hand, many businesses that have focused on selling emotionally appealing products or services have been very successful with their marketing campaigns. They will continue to succeed in the future as long as they keep focusing on their customers' needs and wants at that time.

THE SCIENCE (AND EXAMPLES) OF SOME POWERFUL AND IMPACTFUL EMOTIONAL MARKETING

The reason why emotions are so powerful is that they are what drive our actions. Emotions are what motivate us to take action. You can have all the logical reasons to do something, but you will not take action if you don't feel it emotionally.

Emotion is what drives us to do what we do, and that is why marketing campaigns that use emotion as their currency have been successful in the past and will continue to be successful in the future as well if they continue to focus on creating emotionally appealing products or services for their customers.

Emotions are not only powerful, but they can also be a potent and effective marketing tool. One of my favorite examples of using emotions effectively via marketing is the movie "Field of Dreams" by Universal Pictures (the film itself is a great movie).

The marketer (Universal Pictures) used the emotion of hope to help them sell their movie to the public. Their marketing campaign used the feeling of hope by using the slogan "If you build it (meaning a baseball field), he will come." This helped people to desire the product (the movie) because they wanted something that would give them hope in life. This is one of my favorite examples of emotional marketing because it is so effective at getting people to buy your product or service.

I am not saying that you should use this example when marketing your products or services, but I am saying that you should use some emotional appeal in your marketing campaigns. You want your marketing campaigns to be as emotionally appealing as possible, so you can get your target market to buy from you and not your competition.

A BRIEF INSIGHT INTO THE "DARK PSYCHOLOGY" OF EMOTIONAL MARKETING (WITH EMPHASIS ON THE POSITIVE AND PRODUCTIVE USE OF SUCH TACTICS)

Emotional marketing can be considered "dark" because it uses psychological tactics that play on people's emotions to help them sell their products or services to the public. This is not necessarily a bad thing when used properly, but some people do take advantage of people by using emotional marketing in an unethical and unfair way to their target market.

However, as long as you are positively using emotional marketing and not taking advantage of people's emotions, it can be a potent marketing tool. Therefore, my philosophy is to always use an emotional appeal in marketing and positively benefit my target market.

I genuinely believe that when you help your target market get what they want, then they will not only come back to buy from you again, but they will also tell their friends about how you helped them get what they wanted. This is the way the marketplace works. You help people get what they want, and you will be successful in the market.

Emotions are robust and powerful tools for marketing because of their power to motivate people to take action and make them do what you want them to do by using positive emotional appeals in your marketing campaigns.

Introducing Fear - The Ultimate Emotional Marketing Tool

Fear is a compelling emotion that can be used to help you sell your products and services to the public. Fear is usually considered one of the most powerful emotions because it will cause you to protect yourself from whatever you are afraid of. For example, suppose you are afraid of losing your job or being hurt. In that case, you will be motivated to prevent those things from happening.

Fear is also a very emotionally appealing emotion because it makes people feel fear. It makes them want something to help them avoid feeling that fear or protect them from whatever they are fearful of. So if you use the right kind of fear in your marketing campaigns, you can be sure that your target market will buy something from you to get rid of their fear, or they will buy something from you to protect themselves from whatever they are fearful of about.

In short, fear is not only an effective marketing tool, but it is also an effective emotional marketing tool because it can help you sell your products and services in a dynamic way that helps people get what they want (to either avoid feeling fear or to get rid of their fears). When appropriately used, fear can be used as an effective marketing tool that your target market will be willing to buy from you.

Fear is one of the most powerful emotions out there because it can drive people to take action. If you are afraid of losing your job, then you will take action to keep your job. If you are afraid of being hurt, you will protect yourself from being damaged. If someone uses fear effectively in their marketing campaigns, they can be very successful if they use it correctly.

Fear is one of the most powerful marketing tools out there because it can be used to help sell your products and services to the public by using it as an emotional appeal that explores their fears and how your products or services can help them get rid of those fears or protect themselves from whatever they are fearful about.

THE FUTURE OF MARKETING IS DRIVEN BY EMOTION - HE WHO CAN MASTER THE TACTICS OF EMOTIONAL MANIPULATION WILL SUCCEED.

Marketers should be able to develop marketing strategies that attract people to buy, not just to do business with you.

Be able to understand and analyze people's emotions and feelings, which will allow them to create more persuasive marketing messages.

Before you start thinking of the successive best marketing campaign, ask yourself if your message has the right emotional tone. The key is to think from the perspective of the consumer, not your own.

You can't just market your product or service in a vacuum - it has to be meaningful to them, given their existing state of mind. You have to create a "love mark." Emotionally driven products have higher retention rates than those sold on rational grounds. People are more likely to remember an experience that makes them feel something rather than one that is just functional. Emotion is everything, because it drives everything else. You can't create emotion unless you understand what it means to the people you are trying to reach - only then can you evoke it in them when you talk about your product or service.

Emotions are contagious - they spread through society like a virus through a population, but they're not necessarily new emotions - they're shared experiences or memories that remind us of something we've felt before but forgotten how we felt about it when we experienced it for real. Recreating this emotion triggers our memory of the original experience - the feeling itself is not created; it is remembered.

Sensory experiences trigger memories, so you need to understand how consumers think and feel to create an emotional response to trigger a memory. The five senses are sight, sound, taste, smell, and touch.

Emotions occur when we share an experience with other people - it's not just how it makes us feel, but "how" we think that makes it an emotion. It must be something beyond just a sensation or feeling, but which has meaning for us - otherwise, it's just a reaction; we don't feel anything about it. When the surface has meaning for us, we think about it - we imprint the emotion upon our memory. We can share feelings through music, art, and stories (and marketing). Empathy is at the root of all emotions; when another person can empathize with you (understand what you're going through), they'll be able to create a connection with you and share your feelings - they'll become invested in your story.

Hence, the future of marketing is about creating stories that evoke emotions in the consumer. Marketing has always been about telling stories, but the difference now is that it's about telling emotional stories and helping people make emotional connections with your product or service.

The most crucial thing in marketing is to build a relationship with the consumer. If you can do this, you can build an emotional foundation for your product or service - from there, and you can create a story that will trigger a memory of that emotion in the consumer. The story triggers the memory; the memory evokes an emotional response and makes them want to buy your product or service.

3

MARKETING THROUGH THE AGES

It's important that we take a look at the history of marketing before we dive further into the future of marketing, as we are doing in this book. We need to understand how marketing has evolved, what worked and didn't work, and what the changes are that have occurred over time. The best way to do this is to take a look at the history of marketing through the ages.

WHERE DID MARKETING BEGIN

The earliest recorded examples of marketing can be traced back to around 4000 BC. At that time, the Sumerians were one of the first civilizations to use a primitive form of marketing. They used marketing to sell their goods and services in a type of bartering system. The Sumerians would buy goods from other civilizations or societies and then use that good as an item for trade with others.

The Egyptians completely revolutionized the way we do business by developing one of the most well-known business practices: advertising. The Egyptians are responsible for constructing some of the world's most prominent landmarks, including The Great Pyramids at Giza, designated as "Advertising Monuments" by historians.

Throughout history, each civilization has innovated methods and strategies to help businesses grow and prosper through various marketing forms. It has been said that marketing started as a system for sharing information about products with potential customers and evolved into a system for selling products using various media forms to reach consumers and potential customers. As society evolved, so did marketing strategies; but it wasn't until around 1920 when advertising truly flourished—with people like John Wanamaker and Claude Hopkins—that we saw the beginnings of modern-day marketing.

The Golden Age of Marketing:

The next significant turning point in marketing came with the introduction of television in the 1950s. At this time, marketing began to focus on reaching the masses using mass media. The population in the United States was growing, and television was the perfect outlet to get this growing group of people.

It seemed as though anything was possible during this time period: if you built it, they would come. The idea that if you simply advertise your product enough, you would make a sale was the prevailing thought at the time. As such, there was much emphasis placed on effective advertising campaigns to sell your products and services to the masses.

When television was first introduced as a way for businesses to reach their customers, companies invested millions of dollars in television advertising. At that time, people were more inclined to tune into their local TV news or entertainment shows than they were to read a newspaper or magazine advertisement.

When did people begin to focus on and build specific marketing strategies actively:

The next significant turning point in marketing came with the introduction of the Internet in the 1990s. At this time, marketing began to focus on reaching people with a specific strategy or message through various channels on the Internet. The population in the United States was growing, and advertising on the Internet was a great way to reach these potential new customers.

As we moved into the new millennium, our attention turned to social media networks as a way for businesses to reach their customers. People were spending more time using social media networks than watching TV or reading newspapers and magazines.

The most recent significant turning point in marketing came with the introduction of mobile marketing in the 2000s. At this time, marketing began to focus on reaching people through various channels on their mobile devices. The population in the United States was growing, and people were spending more time using mobile devices than they were watching TV or reading newspapers and magazines.

THE ERAS OF MARKETING

Although there are many different eras of marketing, there are five that stand out.

1. The Print Era:

During this era, the only way to market products was through print ads in newspapers and magazines. The only information a consumer would be able to get about your products is what you told them. This is also the time when companies were named after their founders or owners. Today this is not the case, as many companies are named after their products instead.

In the print era, many companies started to use slogans. An example of a marketing slogan is "Just Do It" by Nike.

2. The Radio Era:

In the 1920s, the radio became popular, and marketers quickly jumped on board. During this time, the ads for products were more focused on the product than the company and were often very entertaining and funny.

3. The Television Era:

This is the era we are in today. Now, marketers have more access to consumers and spend billions of dollars per year on advertising and marketing. Modern-day marketing is a bit more simple than it was in the past. There are so many different types of mediums that marketers can use when trying to reach consumers.

4. The Digital Era:

So far, this is the most recent era of marketing. The digital age has only really been around since 1995, when the first smartphones were released. It wasn't until 2004 that there was a massive increase in smartphone sales. Now, marketers have more access to consumers than ever before.

Today, marketers can use social media, google AdSense, paid search, and more to reach consumers with their marketing campaigns.

5. The Discovery Era:

This is the upcoming era of marketing. In this era, marketers will have even more access to consumers. They will have even better ways of reaching out to those consumers. We will also see many new products launched that we have never seen before, such as virtual reality and self-driving cars. If you are a marketer, you need to pay close attention to this new era as it will change everything in the marketing world!

NOW, TAKE A LOOK AT THE MOST SIGNIFICANT MILESTONES IN THE EVOLUTION OF MARKETING.

1895: The Furrow by John Deere

The birth of content marketing starts with John Deere. The Furrow was an instruction book on how to operate the farm machinery of the time. It was also a catalog of products you needed to get your job done. The Furrow sold over 5,000,000 copies in its first year and made John Deere a household name. The Furrow helped acclimate farmers to the idea that they could buy their farm equipment rather than making it themselves.

John Deere revolutionized farming by making farmers into consumers. In 1955, the John Deere company had over 10,000 employees and nearly 3,000 dealers.

1922: Sears launches World's Largest Store radio program

The first radio program was designed to sell. The program was about the world's largest store. The store sold everything and anything you needed for your home. The radio program gave people a reason to head to the store and buy things they need for their homes.

The 1930s: Procter & Gamble (P&G) begins to foray into radio with serialized dramas

The first soap operas were developed by Procter & Gamble to sell soap. The soap operas were all about radio families and the problems they faced. They were so popular that they were adapted into books and movie series. The soap operas helped P&G to become a household name. Procter & Gamble would go on to purchase radio stations, so they could broadcast their soap operas.

1950–1980: Mass media takes hold

The 1950s and 1960s saw the rise of mass media. This was a time of television, radio, billboards, and magazines. There were more people in America than ever before. With this explosion in population came a boom in the media. The boom in media led to an explosion of advertising.

This was also a time of two-way communication between consumers and companies. The rise of radio, television, and magazines allowed companies to communicate directly with their customers. This created a sense of intimacy between the consumer and the company. Companies and consumers could talk to each other.

This intimacy would serve as the precursor for the modern-day marketing landscape.

2004: Microsoft launches the first primary corporate blog

Microsoft launched the first blog from a major corporation. The blog was called MSN Spaces, and Bill Gates wrote it. The blog was all about the future of computing. It also offered a glimpse into the inner workings of Microsoft. The blog would go on to become one of the most popular blogs on the Internet.

The launch of this blog was a significant milestone in marketing history because it established blogs as an essential part of the marketing landscape. Gates saw that blogs were more than just a way to communicate with customers; they were an opportunity for companies to develop relationships with consumers.

And in the past 20 years, the change has been so fat and frequent it even feels hard to keep up at times:

The rise of digital content

The creation of blogs, podcasts, and video channels

Ads becoming more targeted and personalized.

Social media changing the way we interact with brands

Google's algorithm has been updated 500+ times since 2000. That's more than one update every three months for 18 years!

CHANGE IN THE PAST 20 YEARS

In the past 20 years, the marketing industry has undergone a complete change. Many marketing channels and methods have also disappeared.

From 2000 to 2010, the marketing industry has witnessed many changes in terms of channels and methods of marketing. Most of them have disappeared since then.

In fact, the rise of social media over the last few years has already made most traditional channels disappear.

Magazines

The decline of magazines started in the year 2000. The reasons for the decline are many. Since its inception, the digital revolution has given rise to many new media platforms and advertising methods, including Facebook, YouTube, Google AdWords, and Twitter. In addition to the increased competition from these new media channels, magazines have lost readership because of declining interest in reading newspapers and magazines.

Newspapers

Newspapers have been declining from 2010 onwards. Declining newspaper readership is a fact that is known to everyone across the world. In India, it is even more pronounced due to the rise of electronic media platforms like TV and the Internet as a source for news. This decline is that newspapers have not adapted to changing trends in people's lifestyles and demands. This has resulted in people shifting their preference towards other news sources like e-newsletters and online news portals instead of going for print editions of newspapers.

Television commercials

Television commercials have been an important marketing channel since their beginning in the 1950s in various countries worldwide, including India and abroad like America, etc. However, they have been on a decline from 2004 onwards due to several reasons.

One of the main reasons for this decline is the increased competition from newer media channels. People are now spending more time on TV and less on the Internet and cable TV compared to 2004. This has resulted in people shifting their preferences towards newer media channels like YouTube, Facebook, Twitter, etc.. which offers a more exciting experience and also allows people to share their views on the content with other users. In addition to this, many other factors have led to this decline – increased competition from direct mailers, and emails.

Direct mailers

Direct mailers have been steadily declining since 2000 due to the increased usage of the Internet and emails by people. People have also found them to be expensive as compared to other marketing methods.

Emails

Email marketing is a method used by companies across the world to reach their customers. It can be a very effective way of marketing but has its drawbacks as well as limitations. Today, most people check their emails on their phones or tablets and not using computers on which they used to receive emails earlier. This has led to a decline in the number of emails being opened by people and is now only used by marketers who want to create relationships with customers using it for newsletters.

CHANGE IN THE PAST TEN YEARS

If you thought that the changes from 2000 to 2010 were massive, wait till you see what has happened in the past ten years from 2011 to 2021.

The rise of social media

Social media marketing has done for companies what television commercials were doing in the past. They have given companies a platform to reach out to millions of people across the world. This is one of the most important marketing channels and is used by companies around the globe to reach out to millions of people.

Search engine marketing

Internet advertising has also seen a significant change in the last ten years. Search engine marketing (SEM) is one of the essential Internet advertising formats that marketers worldwide use to reach out to millions of people. Since 2011, SEM has seen an increased usage across the world. In fact, Google alone accounts for more than two-thirds of all searches in India. This has resulted in a massive increase in websites being created by companies worldwide and a massive increase in search queries being made by people on Google.

Influencer marketing

Social media has also given rise to the concept of influencer marketing. In this, marketers use influencers to promote their products and brands. An influencer is defined as an individual who has many followers on social media and can influence people's purchase decisions on social media. This concept is used widely by companies worldwide to promote their products and brands on social media.

Mobile apps

Mobile apps have also seen a significant rise in usage in the last ten years. Mobile apps are now being used by people worldwide for various purposes, including reading news, listening to music, shopping online, etc. In fact, there are more than 2 million apps available across multiple app stores today that can be downloaded by people onto their phones or tablets, which they can then use for various purposes. Apart from that, companies have also started using mobile apps as marketing tools to reach out to millions of people worldwide, using them for marketing purposes like creating applications, and many more.

Social bookmarking sites

Social bookmarking sites like LinkedIn, Twitter, and Facebook have been used very effectively by marketers worldwide to create brand awareness and increase traffic on their websites through social bookmarking sites by sharing content on them. In fact, most of these social bookmarking sites have been used by companies across the world to create brand awareness and increase traffic on their websites.

LOOKING AT CHANGE YEAR BY YEAR IN THE PAST DECADE (EMPHASIZING HOW RAPIDLY THINGS CAN CHANGE AND THAT ONE NEED TO BE READY FOR ADAPTATION)

2011:

Social Media began to gain traction, with Twitter and Facebook leading the way. The social media platforms were seen as a great place to connect with people and build a stronger personal brand. The tools of the trade were still blogs, YouTube, and forums (e.g., Warrior Forum), to name a few.

Mobile-first started to take off as smartphones became more popular, especially among younger generations. In 2011, the iPhone 4s came out with Siri being one of its strongest selling points. This was also around the time that Apple's App Store began to gain traction and Android, which was well on its way to becoming a dominant mobile platform.

2012:

In 2012, the world got a little more complex, and social media really came into its own. Facebook became the dominant social media platform with over 1 billion users by 2012. Twitter was still growing but was not nearly at Facebook's level yet. Google+ began to make headway as well and was seen as a great way to connect with influencers in your niche (although it never really gained traction as it should have).

Another significant milestone is that Google started to pull back on SEO which caused many people in the SEO industry to lose their jobs. This was somewhat due to their Penguin algorithm update, which essentially made it much harder for spammy sites to rank and gain traffic. This led many people in the SEO industry to change their focus, especially those who were making money through black hat techniques (e.g., link building).

2013:

In 2013, we saw the emergence of several new marketing strategies, including growth hacking and conversion rate optimization (CRO), among other things. Growth hacking became a popular term around 2013 due to companies like Dropbox, which were growing very quickly despite not having as much funding as they would have liked from venture capitalists. Growth hacking worked for them because they used different ways of getting customers, such as viral marketing, offering referral programs, and getting featured in the press.

Conversion rate optimization also became widespread as marketers realized that there were ways to make their landing pages more effective by tweaking certain elements (e.g., the copy and the design). This led to a strong focus on A/B testing, which is still popular today.

2014:

Growth hacking continued to be very important in 2014, and so did conversion rate optimization. SEO also continued to be a big focus, but it was a bit different than before. SEO in 2014 was all about content marketing and creating valuable content for your audience. Everyone started to create blog posts, infographics, and videos to rank for keywords which helped them get more traffic and leads.

2015:

In 2015, the biggest thing that hit the marketing world was the emergence of live video streaming platforms like Periscope and Meerkat. These platforms allowed people to go live on camera as they saw fit. They were able to build a following of loyal followers who loved watching them stream live. This was especially popular among celebrities who could use these platforms to interact with their audiences personally while also getting free publicity thanks to all of the channels covering them (e.g., sports channels).

2016:

In 2016, products like Pokemon Go became very popular because they used augmented reality (AR) technology within their app so people could catch Pokemon in real life using their phone camera. Snapchat emerged as another popular platform because it allowed people to send self-destructing messages that were only viewable for a short amount of time after being sent (no one else could see them unless they took a screenshot). This caused some controversy when it was discovered that people were using the platform to send inappropriate images to each other.

2017:

In 2017, we saw the introduction of chatbots (essentially automated messaging systems), which became very popular in online stores because they allowed people to do things like ask questions and get answers without waiting for customer support representatives. In addition, there were many new live-streaming platforms, such as Facebook Live, which allowed people to go live on Facebook and gain followers from the social media giant.

There was also the growing popularity of voice-activated home assistants like Google Home, allowing advertisers to collect even more data about consumer habits offline.

2018:

In 2018, virtual reality (VR) began to enter the mainstream as companies like Oculus Rift and Samsung Gear VR started offering affordable devices with enough quality and graphical power to provide a good VR experience. We also saw 3D printing become much more popular as companies like MakerBot released 3D printers that were affordable for most consumers ($1,000-$3,000). A new trend also emerged around this time called Cryptocurrency, where people could earn money by mining digital currencies such as Bitcoin. In addition, crowdfunding became very popular due mainly to all of the success stories from successful Kickstarter campaigns.

2019:

In 2019, blockchain technology became more popular as it gained much attention from the media because of Bitcoin and Ethereum. Blockchain is basically a decentralized digital ledger that is used to verify transactions between two parties. It is currently precious for things like Cryptocurrency. Still, in the future, it could be used for a variety of applications, from medical records to voting systems.

2020:

In 2020, we saw the rise of AI (artificial intelligence), which is the ability for machines to become more intelligent than humans. For example, think about how much smarter Siri has evolved since its launch in 2011. The same goes for self-driving cars and many other things that AI algorithms will power in the future. In addition, we saw VR become even more mainstream as companies such as Oculus started to release their own VR headsets that were even more affordable ($200-$400). In addition, AR also got even better thanks to Apple releasing their iPhone 8, which had ARKit built into it, which made it possible for people to experience augmented reality on mobile devices along with a lot of other cool features like Emojis (animated emojis).

2021:

In 2021, there will be some significant changes, including the rise of blockchain technology which will be used for various purposes such as smart contracts, Cryptocurrency, and medical records. AI will continue to advance as well, but it is expected to start advancing at a much faster pace than before. In addition, some experts are predicting that we will begin to see the rise of virtual reality hardware that is affordable for everyone (e.g., Google Cardboard).

Over the next ten years, I think it's safe to say that we will see many different changes in marketing and advertising. The main thing that one must do to succeed over the next decade is to adapt your marketing strategies based on what is currently going on and what you think could be coming about shortly. Marketing is an ever-changing industry, and many new trends come back every year. It's essential to pay attention and adapt accordingly because if you don't, you might get left behind!

As you can see, many changes have occurred over the past decade. They will continue to occur over the next decade in marketing and advertising. It's essential to keep an eye on these changes and adapt accordingly to succeed in this industry! This brings us to the next chapter, where we learn about the mistakes often made in marketing and how you can avoid making these mistakes.

4

AVOIDING THE MOST COMMON MISTAKES

This chapter will focus on the most common mistakes made by small businesses when they attempt to market their business. By avoiding these mistakes, you can be assured of marketing success for your business.

Here are the 100 reasons **why** the market is not seeing your marketing compiled from the top experts in the Internet Marketing industry.

1. THE MARKET HAS NO CLUE YOU EXIST.

You are not targeting the right market, and your marketing is not targeting the market that is most likely to buy from you. If you don't know who your market is, how can you market to them?

To avoid this mistake, decide exactly what demographic you are targeting. Then learn everything you can about their lifestyle, interests, habits, etc. Even if you are selling a commodity product (a product that everyone needs), there are still differences in how different demographics buy and use the product.

For example, dogs need dog food, but there are many different types of dog food available. Some dogs like to eat out of a bowl on the floor, while others like to eat from a can on a countertop. Dog owners also have different lifestyles and attitudes toward their pets which are reflected in their buying habits and product preferences. You could be selling dog food, but you could also be selling a lifestyle.

2. THE MARKET NEVER EVEN HEARD OF YOU.

No one knows about your business. As a result, you are not marketing effectively to the market you targeted.

To avoid this mistake, you need to find out how to get your market's attention. You need to be creative and innovative in your marketing ideas. Once you have their attention, you must be able to persuade them to visit your website or at least call you for more information.

3. YOU ARE NOT IN A POSITION TO BE KNOWN.

You have no authority, credibility, or trust with your market. To avoid this mistake, you must earn the trust of your market before they pay attention to you.

For example, if you are selling cars, you must be a car expert. You must know everything about cars. Then you will be in a position to speak with authority about the vehicles you sell. People will then trust that what you say is true and will want to do business with you.

4. YOU ARE NOT IN A POSITION TO BE HEARD.

Your market has no reason to listen to you. You have not earned their trust, you don't have credibility, and you don't know enough about your market to be able to speak with authority.

To avoid this mistake, you must first earn the trust of your market. This will give you the authority to speak on their behalf. Then, when they are interested in hearing what you have to say.

5. YOUR MESSAGE IS NOT CLEAR, NOT CONSISTENT, AND NOT COMPELLING.

You don't know what you want your market to see, you don't know how you want to say it, and you don't convey it consistently and compellingly.

To avoid this mistake, you need to know your message very well. You need to know exactly what you want your market to know about your business. You need to say it in one sentence and then repeat it throughout your marketing to be clear and consistent.

6. YOUR MESSAGE IS NOT ATTRACTIVE TO THE MARKET.

Your marketing message is not attractive to the market that you want to attract. This can be caused by a poor message or a lack of a message.

To avoid this mistake, learn the art of "storytelling" and how to create compelling stories that attract the market you want. Marketing messages are real stories, and most people love to hear stories. If you don't know how to tell a compelling story, hire someone who does or takes a course in business storytelling.

7. NOT ENOUGH PEOPLE HEAR YOUR MESSAGE.

You have a compelling message, your market knows about it, but they don't know about it because not enough people hear your message.

To avoid this mistake, hire the services of an experienced marketing professional to build you a marketing campaign that includes various forms of media (TV, radio, Internet, etc.) and is targeted to get your message out to the most people possible within your budget.

8. PEOPLE DO NOT BELIEVE YOU.

Your message is attractive, your market hears about it, but they don't believe you because they can't see the proof or they don't trust you.

To avoid this mistake, be prepared to back up every claim you make with proof and testimonials. For example, ensure that all your website pages have testimonials from happy customers and include a particular page with links to positive endorsements from other websites or people in the media, if possible.

9. PEOPLE ARE NOT MOTIVATED TO TAKE ACTION.

Even if they believe you and your message is attractive, your market does not take action because they are not motivated.

To avoid this mistake, make sure that the people who see your message are motivated to take action by offering a special deal, gift, or some other form of incentive to make them act now.

10. NOT TRACKING RESULTS

You don't know what is working and what isn't. You are not tracking the results of your marketing campaign.

To avoid this mistake, you need to track all your marketing efforts by setting up a Google Analytics account on your website. This will provide you with a detailed statistical analysis of how many people come to your website, from where they came, where they went, and what they did when they got there.

Of course, you will also need to set goals and objectives for every marketing activity. Your tracking results will help you determine if you are reaching your goals and objectives.

11. IGNORING PRODUCT DEVELOPMENT

You are not developing new products, services, or features to sell to your existing customers. You are not trying to find the next need in your market and then create products or services that meet that need.

To avoid this mistake, take some time to brainstorm and develop new product and service ideas. Then create a plan for testing those ideas and developing the ones that are most likely to succeed in your market. Just because an idea is a good idea does not mean it will be successful. You have to test and refine the concept until you know it is a winner.

12. NOT TESTING IDEAS

You do not spend any time measuring the success of your marketing efforts. You don't track who is visiting your website, how they are finding you, how they interact with your marketing and sales materials, what is working, and what is not working. You don't track conversions, and you don't track your costs.

To avoid this mistake, create a website tracking system that will tell you how many visitors you have, where they came from, where they go on your site, how much time they spend on each page of your site, and which pages they visit most often.

Spend some time analyzing the data for trends that can help improve your marketing efforts in the future.

13. FAILING TO DISTINGUISH YOURSELF

You are not differentiating yourself from the competition in a way that makes customers see a clear difference between you and the other guys. Therefore, your marketing messages are not differentiating you from the other guys.

To avoid this mistake, create a complete description of your company and your business. Then write down the unique advantages of your business in one of two ways:

1. Write down all the benefits your company offers to customers that nobody else does or can offer.
2. Write down all the things you do better than anyone else.

After completing these descriptions, write out a paragraph about each benefit or advantage that clearly and succinctly explains how it is different from everyone else. Then add this paragraph to every piece of marketing material you create for yourself or your products to give people a reason to choose you over everyone else (remember the next step).

14. FOCUSING ON THE WRONG THINGS

You are spending more time focusing on what you don't do, what you can't do, what you won't do, and why you are different from everyone else. You are spending more time focusing on why your competitors suck instead of spending time focusing on how you can build a better business.

To avoid this mistake, understand that it is not about you. It is about the customer and what the customer wants and needs. Think about how your customers think about your competition. If they have a choice between you or someone else, what things are most important to them? Then focus all of your marketing efforts around those things. If it is price, then focus on price. If it is quality, focus on quality.

15. TRYING TO BE ALL THINGS TO ALL PEOPLE

You are trying to do everything yourself, and you are trying to be all things to all people. But, unfortunately, you do not have a team of people that can help you with marketing, sales, customer service, and product development. So you are trying to do everything yourself.

To avoid this mistake:

- Create a complete description of your company's actions and what it is good at doing.
- Break down those descriptions into the specific tasks that need to be done.
- Find people who are good at doing those particular tasks and put them in charge of the job. This will give

you more time to focus on the things only you can do and will provide you with more time to focus on marketing and sales.

16. UNCLEAR & CONFUSING MESSAGING

Your marketing messages are unclear, confusing, or not believable. You don't have a consistent message, and it is not clear to customers what you sell and the benefits of your products or services. Your sales materials look like everyone else's, but they do not clearly explain how you are different from the competition.

To avoid this mistake, make sure your website, blog, logo, and marketing materials all have the same consistent theme and communicate one clear message to your customers about the benefits of your products or services. In addition, make sure that every piece of your marketing material is communicating your unique value proposition to the customer. (This is a different message from everyone else, which makes customers want to buy from you instead of someone else.)

17. LACK OF AUTHENTICITY

You are not authentic. You are trying to be someone or something you are not. You are trying to be like someone else who is successful in your market. You are trying to fit in with the crowd and not stand out from everyone else. You are not true to yourself.

To avoid this mistake, create a complete description of your company and your business and how it is different from everyone else in your market (see the steps above for defining yourself). Then write down what makes you, you.

If you are not authentic, you are not truthful to your customers. Your customers will sense this and will not trust you.

18. NOT PARTICIPATING IN THE CONVERSATION

You are not participating in the conversation. You are not a part of the conversation that is going on about your market and your industry. You are not a part of the conversation that is going on about your customers. If you aren't a part of the conversation, you will be left out when making the buying decision.

To avoid this mistake, participate in all conversations related to your industry and customers. For example, participate in blogs, comment forums, chat rooms, etc. Please make sure all your employees know how important it is to participate in these conversations and do so regularly and passionately.

19. ANALYSIS PARALYSIS

You have done too much analysis and have not taken any action. You have spent so much time thinking about your marketing, and you have decided that there is no way you can be successful at marketing, so you have given up. You are waiting for the perfect time to market, and that will never come.

To avoid this mistake, take action now! The longer you wait, the more time your competitors will have to gain an advantage over you.

20. RISK AVERSION

You are afraid to take a risk. You are afraid to try something new. You don't want to make a mistake because of what people might think of you or how it might affect your company or business reputation. But taking no action is definitely a risk, and if it doesn't work, it could mean the end of your company or business.

To avoid this mistake, take action now! The longer you wait, the more time your competitors will have to gain an advantage over you.

21. VANITY METRICS

When vanity metrics are used, the business owner measures the wrong things and basing their decisions on those metrics.

For example, when you post something on social media but there are no likes or comments, you might think that the post was a failure. Or, if your sales page has a high click-through rate, but very few people actually buy, then you might think the page is a success.

Vanity metrics are often used to measure marketing campaigns and are most commonly used by business owners that don't understand marketing very well. As a result, they choose the wrong metrics to track, and then they don't know why their marketing is failing.

To avoid this mistake, learn which metrics really matter and focus on those.

22. YOU ARE NOT TESTING.

This is a classic mistake that many beginners make. They don't set up a realistic testing schedule, and when they do, they don't stick to it.

Make sure you are testing every aspect of your marketing, from value propositions to headlines, from pay-per-click ads to sales pages. You need to make sure that you are not wasting your time and money on any of those aspects without knowing that they are working.

23. ASSUMPTION BASED PLANNING

This mistake is made when a business owner makes assumptions about their marketing campaign, but doesn't actually test those assumptions. As a result, they are making decisions based on inaccurate information.

For example, if you decide to write a blog post, you assume that it will get plenty of shares and comments. You might be right. But don't make that assumption. Find out first by testing it out with a small audience first (a beta test). And if your hypothesis is correct, then create the blog post using that knowledge.

24. TRYING TO BE PERFECT

This mistake is made when business owners try to be perfect and never launch their marketing campaigns. They don't launch because they are trying to make everything perfect before they do it. The problem with this is that the longer you delay your marketing activities, the longer it will take you to get results.

25. EXPECTING IMMEDIATE RESULTS

The Internet is not a get-rich-quick scheme. It takes time and effort to build a successful online business with real traffic and profits. So if you think that you can get rich quickly by spending just 3 hours per week, you will be frustrated by the lack of results and will give up too soon.

26. FAILURE TO LAUNCH

Many people spend weeks, months, and even years preparing their marketing before they launch it. They research the market, they optimize their website, they create their sales letter. But what good is all that time and effort if you never actually launch your marketing? The longer you spend researching and planning without ever taking action, the longer it will take to build your business. But, conversely, the sooner you launch your marketing, the sooner you will start getting results.

27. PIVOTING TOO OFTEN

Some people get carried away with testing tactics and change marketing often. This is a mistake, especially if a tactic is converting well for you. If you have found a strategy that works and gets good results, don't change it.

It takes time to find out what works and what doesn't. So do not let yourself be influenced by someone else's opinion or by the advice of an expert who hasn't even tested the marketing themselves. Only test tactics that you have already tried yourself and make changes when you see that they are improving results for you, not when someone tells you that they will work better.

28. FEAR OF CRITICISM

This mistake is made when business owners are afraid to put their marketing materials out there because they are worried about what people will say. They might be afraid of negative comments or even criticism from within their own business. Whatever the reason, they don't want to take a chance on getting "rejected" by the market, so they never launch anything.

To avoid this mistake, know that it is normal for people to criticize things, and that is how the market can find truly successful marketing campaigns and products. So listen to the feedback, but don't let it derail you from your goals.

29. INABILITY TO PRIORITIZE

This mistake is made when business owners can't decide which task to do next, or they are trying to work on too many tasks at once. This leads to confusion, stress, and wasted time. As a result, they end up not getting any of their assignments completed effectively. The best way to avoid this mistake is by using a CRM (Customer Relationship Management) tool, such as Infusionsoft or Ontraport. Then you can create different lists in your CRM that will help you prioritize your tasks better and also track your progress.

30. LACK OF IDENTITY

This mistake is made when business owners don't know who they are. They might not know where they fit in the market, who their customers are, or even what their business does. Without knowing these things, it is impossible to create a successful marketing campaign.

To avoid this mistake, start by writing out your elevator pitch. Then ask yourself questions like "Who am I?" "What do I do?" and "What problems can I solve for my customers?". Next, try to answer those questions using specific examples from your personal experience or your customers' experience. Get as detailed as possible and try to explain it in a way that anyone could understand. Then put everything you have learned into an About Us page or a Frequently Asked Questions page. Then you will have your own unique identity, which can help you with your marketing.

31. NO MARKETING BUDGET

You don't have a marketing budget. Or, if you do, you are spending it all on one marketing technique.

If you want to be successful in the market, you need to spend money on your marketing. You might have heard the saying, "Nothing happens until somebody sells something." But, if you are not selling anything or don't have a budget for marketing efforts, how can you expect to make any sales?

When budgeting for your marketing spend, create a realistic budget and include money for advertising, PPC (pay per click) ads, SEO (search engine optimization), social media campaigns, etc.

32. NOT FOCUSING ON WHAT MATTERS

Many pieces of the puzzle go into making your marketing work. The most critical are your offer, your landing page, and the ad or squeeze page that delivers people to the landing page. If you don't have these three things right, there is no way you will be able to convert your traffic into sales effectively.

33. FORGETTING THE HUMAN ELEMENT

It is easy to get caught up in all of the new technology, and this can lead you to forget that people buy from people. If you don't build your business with a real person in mind, it will be impossible for you to connect with customers on a personal level.

34. NO CLEAR CALL TO ACTION

Your call to action is an essential part of your marketing because it tells the market what they should do next. Therefore, your call to action should be clear and direct, so people understand exactly what they need to do next.

This is especially important on your squeeze page because this is where you will capture the contact information of your market.

35. NO URGENCY

Urgency not only helps you to get more sales, but it also helps you to get better quality sales from people who are looking for a solution to their problem right now. Urgency also allows you to get more leads if your market is interested in the product but needs a little more information before they buy. This means that your lead capture form should have a sense of urgency as well.

36. TRYING TO BE LIKE OTHERS

There are many secrets and tricks out there that can help you to get more sales. However, if you are trying to figure out how all of the other marketers are doing it, you will lose your own identity, and no one will believe that you can provide a solution to their problem. So make sure that your marketing is not just like everyone else's because if it is, it will be hard for people to remember who you are or what you have to offer.

37. NOT OFFERING DISCOUNTS

Offering a discount on your product or service is one of the best ways to get more sales because it gives people the opportunity to try before buying. You can also use discounts as a way of giving something away for free and then following up with an email sequence where you offer something more in-depth. For example, give away an ebook for free and then follow up with a phone call or email where you offer to help the customer further.

38. YOU ARE NOT EDUCATING THE MARKET.

If you are marketing a product or service that your market is unfamiliar with, they will have no idea what you are talking about and will quickly leave your site. Therefore, ensure that you clearly explain what you do, whom it benefits, and why they should buy from you.

39. NO SENSE OF URGENCY

Urgency helps people to take action without thinking about it too much. For example, you can create an urgency by telling people that they only have a limited amount of time to take advantage of your offer before it is too late, or that they will lose out on something valuable if they don't take action right away.

40. AVOIDING NEW MEDIA

Focusing on the Internet is the best way to reach your market. Ensure that you are using all of the media available to you, including social media, blogging, and email marketing. If you want to avoid making this mistake, check out all of the marketing tools available and pick at least one of each type to start with. Then work on building your list so you can build traffic and sales through your blog.

41. AVOIDING SOCIAL MEDIA

Social media platforms like Facebook, Twitter etc., are increasingly being recognized as a direct channel to market and a must for any serious marketer. Therefore, you need to be using them if you want to make an impression on your customers and potential customers.

Social Media is not a "second best" type of marketing. However, it's being used by more and more marketers every day, and it's an integral part of any online marketing strategy.

42. NOT TELLING STORIES

Storytelling is one of the most powerful ways to engage with an audience. Good stories give your audience something to relate to, something to imagine, and a way to feel connected to your brand or business.

The Storytellers Handbook says: "Stories provide a way for an audience to step inside your product or service, into the life of another person, into the future and back into the past."

43. FORGETTING TO INVITE OTHERS

You are not inviting others to participate and take part in your product, service, or business. Without your customers or potential customers taking part in what you do, they can't begin to feel connected with you.

44. BEING BORING

You are boring and not saying anything that will get anyone excited about what you do or what you have to offer. Instead, you need to be creating excitement and interest around your products and services to stand out from the crowd.

If you're going to tell a story about something, make sure it's something interesting!

45. NOT COMMENTING ON BLOGS.

Make comments on blogs related to your industry. Commenting on blogs shows your audience that you have something of value to say, that you care about your industry and the market, and that you're taking part in the conversation.

If you leave a comment, make sure it's exciting or valuable to the blog's author.

46. NO LEAD GENERATION SYSTEM

You are not capturing leads for your business. As a result, all of your marketing efforts are going out into a big black hole. You need to have a system in place to capture leads from all of your marketing efforts, so you can follow up with them and turn them into paying customers.

47. SPAMMING

You are spamming everyone on Social Media platforms with useless information about yourself or your business. But, of course, no one wants to read through all of this information unless they are really interested in what you do and why they should buy from you or want to take part in what you offer.

48. NOT RETARGETING

Retargeting follows people around the Internet who visit your website, until they finally decide to take action and buy from you or become a leader in your database. It's following them around with ads related to whatever they were searching for on Google, Facebook, etc., until they finally become a customer and buy from you.

49. NOT IMPLEMENTING SEO

You are not ranking high on the search engines for your keywords. So it would be best if you used SEO to make sure that when people search for something related to what you do, your website comes up on the first page of Google.

50. NO CONTENT STRATEGY

You are not creating enough content for your audience. Without content, there is nothing for people to share, comment on, or link to. Without content, no one will know who you are or what you do.

51. NOT USING SEARCH ENGINE MARKETING.

In the early days of the Internet, marketers could get away without optimizing for search engines. However, when most people start their buying process online, you need to be visible in the search engines.

If you aren't using PPC (pay-per-click) advertising on Google and Yahoo! or submitting your site to directories and RSS feeds, you are not getting the visibility you need.

52. NOT LEVERAGING ON VIDEO MARKETING.

Video marketing is one of the most effective forms of marketing available today. It is also one of the fastest-growing areas of Internet Marketing. With video marketing, you can position yourself as an expert in your field, build rapport with your prospects and help them solve their problems without even selling anything! In addition, you can connect with people on an emotional level that isn't possible through text alone. Video helps build trust and gives you credibility in ways that a simple sales page just cannot match.

You can create videos for your site, syndicate them on popular sites such as YouTube, or use services like Revver to generate revenue from your videos.

53. NOT NURTURING LEADS

The Internet is a great place to find prospects, but it is not a good place to nurture leads and move them along in the sales process. The Internet does not provide enough control to move prospects through the sales funnel. Your website needs to be able to collect information about your prospects and then use that information to make them feel special, offering just the right products and information at just the right time. The Internet is not good at doing this because it cannot read minds! It can only offer what you tell it to offer, in the same way, each time, meaning that prospects see the exact offers (and ads) every time they visit your site.

54. TURNING AWAY GUEST BLOGGERS

If you have an active blog on your website, why not let other people write for you? You will get content for your blog without having to spend hours writing posts yourself. It also gives people a chance to read your website without even needing an invitation – a potential customer reading your website for the first time could be just one of many people reading your blog without being asked.

Guest bloggers offer you extra content, attract more visitors to your website and give you feedback on how to improve your site. It is also a great way to get free publicity.

55. POOR EMAIL MARKETING

Email marketing is one of the most powerful marketing tools available today because it allows you to communicate directly with your prospects and customers. Email marketing provides a way of building trust with potential customers before you even approach them for the first time in person or on the phone. In addition, a well-executed email campaign can provide a massive boost to your business – sending out regular newsletters about new products, special offers, and exciting news can keep your business name in front of your market regularly even if you haven't had any direct contact with them for months!

An email campaign that delivers regular value to your prospects will help build rapport, create trust and encourage sales. Conversely, poorly executed email campaigns will frustrate prospects and make them less likely to buy from you. So make sure that every single email you send is well-written, relevant, and adds value – or don't send it at all!

56. NOT MAKING PEOPLE FEEL SPECIAL.

You have a website, but can you make people feel special on your website? Master the art of making people feel special. Some people are afraid that if they make people feel special, it will mean they have to give a discount. That is not true. You can still make people feel special without giving them a discount.

For example, let's say you have an email list of 500,000 subscribers, and you send out regular newsletters to your list. Instead of using the standard subject line like "Weekly Newsletter", try something like "David's Weekly Newsletter – Learn how to sell more of your products."

57. NO DIRECT MAIL CAMPAIGN

Direct mail (the process of sending out printed mail to your prospects and customers) has been around for years. It has been tried and tested and is still used by many successful businesses today. However, if you are not sending out regular direct mail campaigns, you could miss out on much business. Sending out periodic newsletters, brochures, or letters to your prospects (and even non-prospects) is a great way to stay in touch with your market and let them know about your products, services, or news.

58. NO REFERRAL PROGRAM

If you have a great product or service, why not give your customers a reason to refer it to their friends and colleagues? A referral program is a perfect way to get people involved, spread word of mouth about your business, and build trust with new prospects. It is also a great way to help your existing customers feel valued and rewarded for being loyal to your business.

59. NOT DOING REGULAR CONTESTS & SWEEPSTAKES.

A contest or sweepstakes is a great way to generate interest in your products or services without having to spend much money on advertising. Competitions are also a good way of capturing information about new prospects. If you offer them something for entering the competition (a free report, free product, or discount coupon), they will be more likely to enter their details to receive it. Contests and sweepstakes are also suitable for getting people talking about your products online in places where they usually wouldn't – enabling you to get more visibility for little cost!

60. TALKING TO THE WRONG PEOPLE

If you are going to market your business, you need to know precisely who you are talking to. Trying to sell to everyone is a sure-fire way of nothing of sale. If you don't know who your market is, how can you market to them?

To avoid this mistake, decide exactly what demographic you are targeting. Then learn everything you can about their lifestyle, interests, habits, etc. Even if you are selling a commodity product (a product that everyone needs), there are still differences in how different demographics buy and use the product.

61. NOT FOCUSING ON RETENTION.

Marketing without retention is a waste of money and time. The most important part of your marketing strategy should be to keep your existing customers coming back for more. If you want to make more sales, make sure to keep the ones you have!

To avoid this mistake, focus on the value of your product or service and help the customer achieve their goals. What benefits does it provide that will make them come back? Always remember, people, buy because they want something. You can't sell them something they don't want. So focus on what you offer that will help the customer achieve what they want.

62. DOING IT ALL BY YOURSELF.

You can't do everything by yourself. You need a team of people who are experts at what they do and will support you in achieving your goals. Hire them or outsource as much work as possible to free up your time to do whatever it takes to achieve your marketing goals. You need a team if you want results!

To avoid this mistake, start hiring and outsourcing as soon as possible, especially when times are tough – not when you need help! If you wait until things get so busy that you have no time, you will be paying a premium for service. It is better to hire people and pay them a reasonable salary than paying top dollar when you need help.

63. NOT SETTING MARKETING GOALS.

You can't market effectively if you don't know what you are trying to achieve. You have to know where you are going or how will you get there? You can't hit a target if it isn't there. Plan out the results and the actions that will achieve those results, and then stick with that plan. If it isn't working, tweak it!

To avoid this mistake:

1. Write down all the goals for your marketing strategy.
2. Set specific, measurable goals that can be achieved within a certain time frame (say three months).
3. Break those goals into specific tasks and action steps.
4. Do as much of these tasks yourself as possible but give people responsibility for each job to feel part of the team and have something to do!

64. NOT PROMOTING YOURSELF

The key to marketing is to be where the people you are targeting are. You need to let them know who you are and what you have to offer. If you don't do this, how do they know who you are or what you have to offer? They don't! So get out there and start marketing yourself!

To avoid this mistake:

1. Post a link back to your website on all your social media profiles and ask your friends and family for their help too.
2. Use your website as the hub for everything about you and your products.
3. Ensure that everything is easy to find from your website, so people can learn about who you are and what you offer.
4. Ensure that everything is easy to find from your

website, so people can learn about who you are and what you offer.

65. RUNNING OUT OF MONEY.

Always run a tight ship with cash flow. This means that if it takes $500/month for three months before the returns start coming in, then only spend $500/month! Don't spend more than needed on marketing because if it doesn't work, then this could be all the money gone before the returns start coming in! If things go well, then there will be extra money left over to spend on more marketing.

To avoid this mistake, if you are just starting, then create a marketing budget based on how much money you have to spend and stick with it! If you have extra cash, then put it away for when things get slow in the future. If you are doing well, keep reinvesting the profits back into your business (or save if things go bad).

66. NOT BLOGGING ENOUGH

Blogging is an essential part of any Internet Marketing strategy! The more high-quality content you can provide, the higher your Google ranking will be, and the more visitors will come to your website. On the other hand, your site will suffer a slow death without regular blogging, which means less traffic, and fewer leads for you! So make sure that everything you do is geared towards blogging!

To avoid this mistake, make sure that everything you do can feed into your blog or adds value to what is already there. For example, write 3-5 articles every week (more if possible) and use your social media profiles to promote each new article. The key is always to be adding value to what is already there! So if you have a new book out, create an article about it on your blog. Then promote that article on your social media profiles. There are many ways to use your content to get more traffic to your website, making sure you always share it on social media.

67. NOT HIRING THE RIGHT PEOPLE.

The biggest mistake you can make when marketing your business online is to ignore or downplay the value of building a real business behind what you are doing. Don't think of your website as a separate business. Instead, think of it as an engine for your actual business. Your website should be staffed and funded by real staff that works for your real business. It's not a hobby, and it's not a side project; it's not a part-time job. It's an integral part of your business!

There are so many things that can be done online these days that can impact your bottom line. However, if you don't have the right people running and working on these projects, they will be wasted efforts. There is no point in having great ideas if you don't have the right people to execute them!

68. WRONG SAMPLE SIZE

In the old days, you used to look at the number of people who visited your site and then draw conclusions about how effective your marketing campaign was. This is a very misleading way of tracking success. It's easy to get a high number of visitors, but when you look at what they do on your site, it may not be very successful. For example, there is no point in getting 100,000 visitors to your site if they don't buy anything from you or take any actions on your site, such as signing up for a newsletter or a unique report.

There are two effective ways to measure success: Number of Visitors and Number of Actions. The first one (number of visitors) is easy to measure, but it doesn't tell you much about how successful your efforts are. The second one (number of actions) tells you more about the effectiveness of your marketing, but it's harder to measure because there are many different actions that people can take on your website.

69. NOT TAKING ADVANTAGE OF PAID TRAFFIC.

Paid traffic is one of the most potent ways to reach new customers online and drive massive amounts of traffic to your site (especially if you are just starting). Think about this - would you rather spend $8 every time someone visits your website or get free traffic from search engines? It doesn't take advanced skills to start using paid traffic. You just need to know what to do.

To avoid this mistake, start using paid traffic to build a list of highly targeted subscribers for your business.

70. NOT OPTIMIZING YOUR SITE.

Your site needs to be properly optimized to get the most search engine traffic possible. This means that you need proper title tags, meta descriptions, and plenty of good quality content on your site. It would be best if you also had some social media sharing buttons and a contact page so people can contact you quickly. Make sure everything is working correctly and looking good!

To avoid this mistake, make sure that the website is easy for visitors to find what they want. In addition, it should be easy for them to contact you and share your pages with their friends via social media sites like Facebook, Twitter, etc. Social Media shares are an excellent way to get free publicity for your site!

71. NOT MANAGING YOUR PIPELINE.

You have no system for managing your leads. As a result, you lose out on opportunities to turn them into customers because you are not following them.

To avoid this mistake, set up a system for tracking and managing your leads. Also, keep in touch with your leads regularly, so they don't think you ignore them.

72. BLINDLY FOLLOWING THE CROWD.

You are doing what everyone else is doing and not differentiating yourself from your competitors. You must be different to stand out. If you are competing on price, you will be forced to compete on price alone and lose profit margins. You can't be all things to all people or do something just because everyone else is doing it, if it doesn't make sense for your business. What works for someone else might not work for you. If it isn't broke, don't fix it (unless it's a broken link or broken image).

73. NOT DOING YOUR RESEARCH.

You don't know anything about the market that you want to sell to or who wants to buy from you. You aren't listening to your target market and learning what they need from you and how they want to buy from you. Everyone thinks their product is the next best thing since sliced bread, but if nobody wants it, then no matter how good the product is, you will still fail.

To avoid this mistake, listen to what people are saying in your market. Do they like or dislike products similar to yours? What are their buying habits? Why do they buy the way they do? What do they want from a product that you could provide? Who is your target market, and what do they want from you?

74. NOT TAKING ADVANTAGE OF WORD OF MOUTH.

You aren't asking your customers for referrals and testimonials, and you aren't providing an opportunity for them to give you both. As a result, you could be missing out on much business. Word of mouth is one of the most powerful ways to spread the news about your business.

To avoid this mistake, ask for referrals when your customer is happy with their purchase or service and most likely to say yes. Give them plenty of opportunities to leave a testimonial for you on your website or social media sites; provide them with the information to write something if they want but don't force it on them if they don't want to write anything. You should also ask for reviews on sites like Yelp and Google Places etc., but don't spam or beg – just ask once at the end of a transaction – people are more likely to say yes after a sale than before.

75. NOT REACHING OUT TO INFLUENCERS.

You are not connecting with influencers in your market and asking them for help getting the word out about your business. There are lots of influential people in every niche whom you can partner with. It doesn't matter if you don't know any influencers personally; you can reach out to them as long as you can find them.

To avoid this mistake, make a list of all the "influencers" in your market and start reaching out to them. You can find these people by researching sites like Twitter and LinkedIn or asking your customers for referrals. Then, ask the influencer for their help and give them something of value in return (a free product or service, free promotion, etc.) so they are more likely to say yes.

76. NOT USING TESTIMONIALS

You don't have any testimonials on your website, social media profiles, or other online locations where people can read about how other people feel about your company or products. If you don't have any testimonials on your site, then why would anyone believe that anyone else likes your business? You must have testimonials and reviews on all of these sites if possible – if you don't have any yet, then start asking for them! Testimonials are also great for SEO because Google picks up on them very quickly and ranks them well in search engine results pages (SERPs).

To avoid this mistake, get testimonials from happy customers and put them on all of your online profiles or ask the customer to post their own review on your website or a place like Yelp.

77. NOT BUILDING RELATIONSHIPS

You fail to build relationships with people in your market because you think they won't buy from you or they don't have any money, and it's not worth your time or effort contacting them. However, there is probably someone who wants something from you that would be willing to pay for it but hasn't heard about you yet – if only they knew you existed.

To avoid this mistake:

1. Start to build relationships with the people in your market.
2. Find out what they want from you and make yourself available to them.
3. Please stay in contact with your customers; they might not be ready to buy now, but they may be in the future, and you don't want to lose touch with them. If someone is unhappy with your service or product, reach out to them and fix things before it's too late.

78. TAKING TOO MUCH ADVICE

You are not following the advice of your mentors, family, or friends. You are not applying any of the advice you are getting from others to your business.

To avoid this mistake, you need to apply the advice you get from others to your business. If you don't have a mentor, hire one. If you don't have family or friends who can give you advice, join an online mastermind group to get advice from other like-minded individuals.

79. NOT OWNING YOUR BRAND.

You are not working on your brand because of time and money constraints. You are not establishing yourself as a leader in your niche because you just do what everyone else is doing.

To avoid this mistake, make branding a priority in your business. Even if it means giving up some things in the short term, it will pay off in the long term by helping to build your authority. It will also help protect your business from future competitors who want to run away with it when they see how much money is being made in that niche.

80. NOT KNOWING YOUR NUMBERS.

You have no idea how much money you are spending and making each month. You do not know approximately how many leads and sales per month that represents. You are not applying any tracking system for measuring these numbers and showing them to the team members to understand what's going on with their marketing efforts and make changes where necessary.

To avoid this mistake, you need to know how much money you spend and make each month. You need to know how many leads and sales per month that represents to understand what's going on with your marketing efforts and make changes where necessary.

81. NOT HAVING A CONTENT CALENDAR.

You are not producing new content at regular intervals. You need to create regular content to be able to build an audience and get them to come back regularly.

To avoid this mistake, set up a content calendar or editorial plan. This will make sure you have enough new content for your audience at all times.

82. NOT USING SOCIAL MEDIA MONITORING TOOLS.

You are not tracking what people say about you on social media sites, so you miss out on opportunities to improve your reputation and engage with your customers.

83. NOT USING A CRM SYSTEM.

You are not using a CRM system for managing your contacts, leads, and opportunities. You can't track activity, such as contact information changes or lost opportunities, because of poor records management.

84. NOT HAVING A CONTENT CALENDAR.

You are not producing new content at regular intervals. You need to create regular content to be able to build an audience and get them to come back regularly.

85. NOT HAVING A SET PROCESS.

You are not following a defined process for marketing. Instead, you are making it up as you go along, making everything inefficient and ineffective.

To avoid this mistake, identify your target market and establish a marketing process for them.

86. NO AUDITING PROCESS IN PLACE

You are not checking the progress of your marketing to find out where you are succeeding and where you are falling short. Unfortunately, this means you can't fix your mistakes and improve performance.

87. SEARCHING FOR A SILVER BULLET

You are looking for an unrealistic marketing solution that will work for everyone. Instead, you need to find solutions that fit your business goals, audience, resources, and skills.

To avoid this mistake, do your research and look for solutions that are suitable for your business.

88. NOT LEARNING FROM YOUR MISTAKES.

You are not learning from the mistakes you make in marketing. Unfortunately, this means you will continue making the same mistakes over and over again.

To avoid this mistake, learn from your mistakes and make changes to your marketing strategy and tactics.

89. HIDING BEHIND YOUR BRAND

You are creating content that is not relevant to your audience. You are not talking about what the customers want. The customers are more interested in what you have to say than they are in your brand name.

To avoid this mistake, find out what the customers want and create content that talks about it.

90. UNCLEAR TARGET AUDIENCE

You aren't clear on who your target audience is or how they can be reached. As a result, you could be wasting time and money marketing to the wrong people.

91. NOT BEING RELEVANT TO THE MARKET.

You are trying to sell a product or service that is not relevant to the market. Not just that, you are almost forcing them to buy it. That's not going to work!

To avoid this mistake, research your market first before selling your product or service. Know what they want and then give it to them. Don't force anything on them.

92. NOT RUNNING A CONTROLLED EXPERIMENT.

You are not running any A/B split testing on your site to see which works and which doesn't work. As a result, you have no idea if you are moving forward or backward with your marketing efforts because no data and analysis are involved.

To avoid this mistake, set up an A/B split test on your website and track its results carefully for at least 2 - 3 weeks. This will help you see which route is working better for you and which isn't to get rid of the losing variation and optimize the winning one. For more details, refer to How To Start an A/B Split Test.

93. FOCUSING ON BECOMING AN EXPERT INSTEAD OF HELPING OTHERS

Not many people like talking about their failures, but everyone likes talking about their success stories. If you have a blog or a website, you can use it to help others in your industry and build your reputation as an expert at the same time.

To avoid this mistake, focus on writing content that will help other people in your industry. Give them tips and valuable information that they can use to improve their businesses. This will not only help them, but it will also help you establish yourself as an expert in your niche.

94. NOT READING OTHER PEOPLE'S MARKETING MATERIAL.

You are not taking the time to read other people's marketing material. As a result, you have no idea what topics are trending in the market, so you can jump on board with one of them and get more attention for yourself and your business.

To avoid this mistake, take time out of your busy schedule to read what others are writing about online. You don't always need to write something new when something is already valuable for you to read and learn from. You can also repurpose their ideas into your material or re-write it into better words so that more people can understand it better than before.

95. LOOKING FOR OVERNIGHT SUCCESS

You are looking for overnight success. You want to change your life and business overnight, and you want it now! You're in a hurry to see results, and you want them as soon as possible.

To avoid this mistake:

1. Be patient. You will get there even if it takes time.
2. If you have a system in place, don't just rely on that; put some effort into it as well. Your business won't grow overnight, and neither will your bank account,

but if you keep working at it, you will get there eventually.
3. Don't give up on anything too early because that's when the magic happens!

96. NOT GOING DEEP ENOUGH.

You are not going deep enough with your marketing efforts. You are only focusing on one aspect of marketing when you focus on multiple aspects of marketing at once to see how they work together to make your efforts more effective.

To avoid this mistake, create a balanced strategy for your business instead of just relying on one aspect of marketing alone. Try combining different marketing elements so that they can work together for your success instead of working alone against each other like they usually would if used separately by themselves. For example: combine SEO with Social Media and email marketing to see how they work together to help you get more traffic and sales.

97. FOCUSING ON FEATURE INSTEAD OF BENEFITS

You are not focusing on the benefits of the product or service you are offering, but instead, you are focusing on its features. So you're not selling benefits; you're selling features!

To avoid this mistake, focus on the benefits instead of the features. What is it that makes your product or service better than anyone else's? What are people going to get out of using it? Why should they choose your product instead of others in the market? To find out what they want, do some research using Google's Keyword Planner Tool and read their reviews online to see what they say about your products or services.

98. TRYING TO BE PERFECT INSTEAD OF LAUNCHING.

You are waiting for everything to be perfect before launching a product or service. You don't want to launch anything that is not perfect, but there is no such thing as an ideal product! Time will pass by, and people will forget about your product before you get it right. Don't let this happen. Launch something right now and then tweak it if necessary later on, depending on what the market says about it.

To avoid this mistake, launch a product or service as soon as you can. There will always be time to tweak it later on once you see how the market responds to it and what they say about it. To launch something now and then improve if necessary later on based on what the market tells you. Otherwise, your competitors will take that opportunity away from you before you even get the chance to do so.

99. NOT BEING OPEN TO NEW IDEAS.

You are not open to new ideas and suggestions. You don't want to listen to other people's opinions because you think you know everything already. You only want to hear what people have to say when they agree with your ideas but not when they don't agree with them. That's not going to work for anyone in the long run!

To avoid this mistake, be open-minded when listening to other people's ideas and suggestions. It is possible that their ideas can help improve your business or marketing efforts, so make time for them instead of ignoring them entirely because they may know something about your business or industry that you don't know yet!

100. BEING TOO ATTACHED

You are too attached to your marketing efforts, and you can't take criticism well. You think you know everything, so you don't consider other people's opinions when working on your business because it's just not possible that you could be wrong about anything. You've never been wrong before; why would you start listening to what people have to say now?

To avoid this mistake, learn how to take criticism well. First, understand that if someone is giving criticism about something, it means that they care enough about you and your business enough to want to make it better for you. So instead of taking it personally or getting angry at them, listen carefully and try whatever they suggest for yourself first before dismissing it too quickly if you feel like their suggestion has merit. If not, explain why not and then ask more questions, so they understand your point of view and give recommendations based on what worked for them in the past instead of just assuming that what worked for them will work for everyone else without even trying it out first.

Let's take a look at the top 7 mistakes made and how you can overcome them or ensure they don't exist in the first place.

1. CAMPAIGN OVERSPENDING

Campaign overspending is one of the most common mistakes made by marketers, especially when it's their first time. They spend too much on advertising, over-promote their brand, and as a result, get much traffic but little or no sales.

This is the fault that many marketers make when they are just starting out and trying to figure out what works and what doesn't work to drive conversions. They blindly spend and hope that it will pay off in the end. This is why you see so many entrepreneurs with large social media followers (viral) but have a more challenging time driving traffic to their sites or converting those visitors into paying customers or leads. The same concept holds accurate with paid ads. It's not enough to just set up a campaign and spend much money – you must know where your audience is and where they are most likely to convert.

How To Avoid The Mistake

This problem can be solved by dividing your budget across multiple platforms and channels. This is difficult for entrepreneurs because they like to put all of their eggs in one basket. However, it is pretty beneficial in the long run. For example, if you have one marketing campaign going across four different platforms or channels, you will get four times the results at half the cost.

2. CAMPAIGNS NOT LAUNCHING ON TIME

I can't tell you how many times I've seen this mistake. Marketers will set up a page, write an excellent copy, set up ads, and then just sit on it for weeks, months, even years. The reason is that they are too afraid of launching it and getting feedback from their target audience. They are afraid of hearing what people have to say about their product or service and don't want to deal with any negative comments.

Here's the thing – negative comments are a good thing. It means you are reaching your audience, which in turn means that you have a strong campaign. The other side is that if you don't get any feedback from your target audience, then chances are you are not reaching them, and the campaign is not working.

How To Avoid The Mistake

When you set up a campaign, make sure that you launch it and get feedback from your target audience. Get their honest opinions about your product or service and use that information to tweak or develop new ideas for marketing campaigns.

3. TRACKING AND INTEGRATIONS BREAKING

This is another mistake that can cost you much money. I've seen many marketers try to save money by not getting the correct tracking and integration systems in place and losing many customers. They didn't know how many sales were being made or where all their traffic was coming from.

How to avoid the mistake

The correct tracking system is crucial for business growth. Not only will you be able to see where your traffic is coming from but also how many conversions you are getting from each source. In addition, you can always tweak your campaign based on the data that you are seeing.

The other thing that you can do is get the proper tracking and integrations in place. Of course, you can't go wrong with free options like Google Analytics or Facebook Reports. However, it would be best to make sure that each of your advertising channels and platforms has its own integrations. A good example is when a Facebook campaign runs well, but you see minimal conversion from the campaign on your site. Then you can go into Facebook reports and see where the traffic was coming from. You can then change your ads or landing page to suit that audience better, increasing the conversion rate.

You want to ensure that every element of your marketing campaign flows together seamlessly so that no leads slip through the cracks because there was an error in the tracking or integration.

4. TARGETING THE WRONG AUDIENCES

If you are targeting the wrong audience, then your marketing campaign will not be very effective. Of course, some businesses have reached their target audience through indirect means, but these are few and far between.

Signs it's happening.

- You see much traffic on your website but no conversions from those visitors.
- You know many people engaging with your content but not converting into paying customers or leads.
- You see much traffic on your Facebook page; however, a small percentage of that is converting into leads or customers.

- You are wasting money on paid ads that are not converting into leads or sales.

How to avoid the mistake

You need to do market research and determine who your target customers are to make better decisions on how you should advertise your product or service. If you don't do this research, then your campaign will fall flat on its face before it even kicks off.

The best thing that you can do here is to start by finding out who your target customers are and where they congregate. You can find this out by doing some market research to find out where your target customers like to hang out. Once you have found that information, you can then tailor your advertising campaign to that audience.

5. BROKEN FORMS, LINKS, AND CHECKOUT SYSTEMS

This is another widespread mistake that many entrepreneurs make. They spend money on paid ads, social media marketing, and other forms of online marketing but don't invest in making their conversion funnels better.

How to avoid the mistake

First impressions are essential, and many times, the first impression that a visitor gets is what will determine if they stay or leave the site. If your landing page looks unprofessional, people will go – that's just how it is. To prevent this from happening, you can hire a professional web designer to make your website look friendly and attractive as well as functional.

In addition to making sure that your landing pages and other conversion elements are professional and functional, you must also make sure that your emails don't get the same fate as your landing pages. It is very common for people to receive many emails every day, some of them may be newsletters that they subscribed to, and some may be advertisements that they signed up for.

Email marketing is one of the most effective forms of online marketing but is also one of the least effective if you have many bounces and unsubscribes. This is a massive waste of money and time for both you and your subscribers. Therefore, it's essential to ensure that your emails are correctly set up and routed through an email marketing automation software like Aweber.

Automation software will prevent you from sending out emails to people who have unsubscribed from your list and remove the potential for spam by constantly checking the IP address of your emails. This will also help you increase the number of emails you send out by automatically sending new subscribers to an autoresponder series that will introduce them to your product or service.

6. NOT HAVING A FOLLOW-UP PLAN.

It is very easy for marketers to get carried away with their campaigns and neglect the rest of their leads regarding online marketing. Many entrepreneurs run campaigns just for running campaigns because they think that nothing will happen if they don't do anything. This is a very common mistake that many marketers make and a big reason as to why their campaigns aren't working out.

How to avoid the mistake

To avoid this problem, you must create a follow-up plan that includes activities such as email marketing automation, social media management, and content marketing. This will help you stay on top of your leads and customers so that you can continue to engage them even when your campaign is over.

7. IMPROPER UNDERSTANDING AND MANAGEMENT OF STATISTICS

What is it

This is another common mistake that many marketers make. Most of them focus on the wrong things and end up losing track of what's essential. For example, you may focus on the number of clicks you receive rather than the number of conversions or sales.

This is a common mistake that many marketers make because it's easy to measure. You just open up Google Analytics, check the number of sessions, and then compare it with your initial goal – pretty simple, right? This is why most marketers think they are doing a good job when they are not in reality.

How to avoid the mistake

Tracking goals is an essential aspect of online marketing because it will help you determine what works and what doesn't work with your campaign. This can also help you determine if a particular campaign has been successful or not. It's always better to focus on the lower number because even if you have 100 clicks but only converted a small percentage of them, it would be better to focus on your conversion rate instead of the total number of clicks.

This is what makes analytics so important – it will allow you to focus on what matters and determine which aspects of your campaigns are successful and which need improvement. Many metrics can be tracked, but it is essential to focus on the most important ones for your business. For example, if users abandon your product page before making a purchase, this might be a good metric for you to track.

5

WHAT YOU NEED TO KNOW FOR ULTIMATE SUCCESS

There are some things in life that you can't change, but there are others that you can. When it comes to marketing, there are some things that you can change, but there are others that you can't. The fact is, no matter how much marketing you do, it won't matter if the person isn't looking for your products or services.

You can only control one thing when it comes to marketing, and that is your own attitude. You can't control the economy, and you can't control if people are looking for what you have to offer; you can't control the price of everything you have to sell.

The fact is, there are a lot of different ways to market, but what works the best for you is dependent on you. You'll see that as we move through this chapter, but the big question is: What can you control?

YOU'VE JUST BEEN SHOWN YOUR BLINDSIDES WHEN IT COMES TO MARKETING.

We do not know many things, and we think we have it all figured out, but the truth is that there is more than that you need to know to become successful in your marketing endeavors.

For example, if you are in network marketing, you need to know the proper prospecting method. So you need to start from the very beginning and understand how everything works, and then decide whether it is right for you or not.

You're empowered and ready to move forward.

The truth is that if you know how to become successful in network marketing, you will be way ahead of the rest. You will know what works and what doesn't and everything else in between.

You can apply the right model to your business and create a stable income for yourself and your family.

The best part is that you get to choose how things go in your business, and this is the best way it can be because you are the one who will reap all the benefits from your hard work and dedication.

Once you take action and put everything in motion, there is no turning back…

You have got to develop your very own strategies and finding ultimate success.

You need to find your own way of making the most out of your money, and you need to do it in the shortest amount of time possible. This is how you will be able to make the most out of your business, and once you find success, you will see that it was all worth it.

There is no point in wasting time with things that are not working for you. You know what works and what doesn't, so there is no point in wasting your time with anything else.

You can start from scratch or build on what you have already started, but the truth is that there are only a few things that really work when it comes to marketing. You just need to keep your eyes open for them and then take action.

The most important thing is that you are willing to learn from your mistakes, which is the only way that you will be able to become successful in your marketing endeavors.

Don't be afraid to take chances and make some mistakes along the way, because this is what will help you move forward.

Make sure to go with the knowledge you have and don't be afraid of getting it wrong, because it is the only way you will learn how things work in the real world. This way, there will not be any surprises when it comes to marketing, and you will be able to make the most out of your money by using the best strategies for ultimate success.

But first, it's going to be incredibly beneficial if we first talk to the experts about some of their most powerful and purposeful bits of advice.

YOUR STORY MATTERS!

Storytelling is, in fact, one of the most effective ways to persuade someone to do something. It's what marketing is all about. And it's what we are all doing when we want the market to see our work.

But, storytelling is not enough. There are some basic reasons why the market is not seeing your marketing. Your marketing may be fabulous, but it needs to be known to get results.

There is a scientific explanation of why storytelling is so compelling, and why the market does not see your marketing. We are going to explore it together, and then you will be able to fix your marketing.

But first, let's talk about the importance of crafting a story in your marketing and how it will help you get results.

Storytelling is Important: Why?

Have you ever had a teacher or a professor start her class by talking about herself? For example, she might say something like this: "I was born in a small town in Montana..." or "I grew up on a farm..." or "I went to school at Harvard...." She would tell you about her life story so that she could make you more comfortable with her.

What she was doing was creating a sense of trust and familiarity with her. She was telling her story so that you would know that she wasn't a stranger, and that you knew something about her. Once she established a connection with you, then she could deliver the content of her class.

Your story is the same way. It's your way of building trust and familiarity with your audience so that they will believe what you have to say and see the value in your marketing offer. Again, it's true whether it's an individual story or a brand story. Storytelling is essential in marketing because it connects with your audience and makes them more comfortable hearing your marketing message.

No wonder the most famous brands in the world are all built on a story. Nike is built on their story of "Just Do It," and Apple is built on the story of "Think Different." Starbucks is built on a story of "Creating a Third Place" and Zappo's is built on their mission to "Deliver WOW Through Service." Even Red Bull, which doesn't have an explicit story, has created an aura of mystery around their brand that makes you want to believe them when they say their drink will give you wings.

A strong story is a powerful thing.

COPY IS EVERYTHING!

Storytelling is the key to all great marketing, but it's not enough. As a copywriter, I am constantly telling people that they should be in the business of creating stories and that they should be good at copywriting. But the reality is that most people aren't good at writing.

And for those who are good at writing because it isn't about writing.

Copywriting is more about telling a story in a way that engages your reader. A good copywriter knows that the story is everything. They know how to write well, but they also know how to entice readers with words that will lead them to do what you want them to do.

Most people are bad at copywriting because they don't understand the difference between writing and copywriting. They think they can just change a few words in their posts and make it good enough. However, that's good for nothing for marketing purposes.

A great copywriter doesn't just tell you a story; they create an experience, so you feel as if you are part of the story.

If you can't do this, you need to hire someone who does.

If you want your marketing to work, you need to bring in a copywriter. It's as simple as that. Of course, you can hire one or learn how to write copy for yourself, but if you want your content marketing and social media efforts to be successful, you will need excellent copywriting skills.

Followed closely by aesthetic design

Aesthetics refers to a person's sense of what is beautiful. This sense is used to judge art, fashion, design, and everyday things, such as evaluating a good-looking car. Aesthetics is all about feelings and emotions. It is why you really like something or not.

As a marketer, you can use aesthetics to connect with your audience. And this is one of the ways that you can connect with your audience if you make sure that your marketing strategy has an excellent aesthetic design.

As the saying goes, "Aesthetics is in the eye of the beholder." So this means that if you know your audience, you will be able to make sure that your marketing has an excellent aesthetic design.

Aesthetics is all about feelings and emotions. This is why you like something or not. In fact, if aesthetics harm you, then you will not like it at all.

Aesthetics can be used in many ways, such as in the design of your website, on the color and font you use, and even in that, you are using a good-looking car to promote your product or service.

Aesthetics is important in marketing because it gives a better impression of what you are selling. This is why aesthetics is really important to marketing.

Remember those emotions we were talking about?

You need to be able to spark emotional responses with the words and images you use.

Words are powerful. There is no doubt about it. But the right words can make a big difference in how you feel about a product or service.

It is because of this that writers try to use words that connect with their audience. This is what we call copywriting, and you need to be able to learn copywriting to have a good marketing copy that will connect with your audience so that they are more likely to buy from you.

And when you learn copywriting, you will be able to evoke emotions in your prospects and customers. Emotions are powerful when it comes to marketing because they can stimulate action.

IT'S NOT FREE...BUT IT CAN BE CHEAP

It's not always free, but many times it is (and whether or not it is free, many times it can be cheap). As you become more efficient in your marketing efforts, you will have far fewer marketing expenses. Also, when you use the same marketing idea over and over again, people begin to realize that you are just repetitious. This can actually work against your interests because people will begin to ignore the message.

Yes, but you can use the same marketing idea over and over and over again. If you have a great idea, it will work for you over and over again. A great marketing idea is like a good joke, it is funny once or twice, but if it is repeated too much, people will begin to tire of it and reject it.

There are many ways to make your marketing efforts more effective and less expensive. Some of these are:

1. Use the same marketing idea over and over again, but in different ways.
2. Use a great marketing idea and then apply it to other media (radio, newspaper, TV)
3. Use the same marketing idea with different pictures, and each time you use it, check to see what results are.
4. Use the same marketing idea repeatedly but change some of the wording to appeal to different groups (example: if you are selling a product that helps senior

citizens, advertise in the newspaper for senior citizens…with a headline that is appealing to seniors).

SOCIAL MEDIA! SOCIAL MEDIA! SOCIAL MEDIA!

Everyone is talking about social media, but why is it that you do not see the results? Why is it that you are spending your time posting on Facebook, but there is no engagement?

The reason for this is down to the audience. The audience on social media is not the same as a traditional physical audience.

For example, when you are attending a live show, you know the people in front of you because they have chosen to be there. Unfortunately, this is not the case on social media.

People who follow your brand on social media do so because they have either chosen to or because it's been recommended to them by friends or family. This is not the same as people choosing to be at a live event.

With that said, there is still potential for your content to go viral on most platforms. There needs to be a balance of quality and quantity for you to see positive results from your social media posts. You need an understanding of how to engage with the audience on social media.

We will discuss ten reasons why your marketing is not working on social media. We will also provide you with solutions on how to solve these problems when you are trying to market your business.

Reason #1: You are not using the right platform for your demographics.

The first reason why your marketing is not working on social media is that you are using a platform that does not fit your demographics.

For example, if you are a youth brand, you should be posting on Instagram and Snapchat instead of LinkedIn or Facebook. If you sell products that appeal to specific age groups, then it makes sense for you to focus on those platforms specifically. There is no point in spreading your content across multiple platforms.

By spending time on a platform that does not relate to your audience, you waste valuable time that could be better spent on media tailored to your demographic.

Reason #2: You're not targeting mobile

The second reason why your marketing is not working on social media is that you are not posting to a mobile audience.

The majority of social media use is done on mobile as opposed to desktop. Therefore, you need to ensure that you are posting to a mobile audience. Some social media platforms allow you to post directly from your phone, but others do not. Therefore, it is essential for you to find out how you can post from the app to be seen by the mobile audience.

If your content is only posted on the desktop, it will miss out on a massive percentage of the audience who are using their phones. Unless the platform allows for direct posting from the phone, then it is best practice for you to upload your image or video, then share it from the app you use on your phone.

Reason #3: You're not posting often enough

The third reason why your marketing is not working on social media is that you are not posting enough.

You need to post regularly and consistently. Do not post just once a week. This will cause your followers to unfollow you, and your brand will become inactive. You want to have an active profile that is updated regularly so that people feel like they should be following you for their daily dose of content. If you are posting once a week, people will assume that there is no point in following you because it does not look like anything new will be shared within the next seven days.

KEEPING CUSTOMERS IS ESSENTIAL - YOU CAN'T JUST "LAND THEM" AND THEN MOVE ON.

The main reason for retaining customers is the same as the reason for acquiring them: it costs less to do so. The cost of acquiring a new customer can be 20 times that of retaining an existing one. It's more expensive to acquire customers than to keep them. Every customer is worth money, and you want to hold onto your customers as long as you can.

Don't just focus on the acquisition - keep your eyes on the retention. Your goal is to get customers to stick around for years, not just a few months.

Most marketers understand this truth, but many of them still focus on acquiring new customers at the expense of the existing ones. They are caught up in an endless cycle of chasing new customers, and they never stop to stop and recognize that these customers are more likely to churn than to stay. Constantly chasing new customers is expensive, and it's time-consuming.

In some cases, it's better to acquire the same customer five times than it is to go after a new one once. It costs a lot less to service repeat customers than new ones. After all, you already have the systems in place to serve them, so why not?

The bottom line is that keeping your existing customers around makes you money. So it's your job to make sure they stay. And that means building trust, loyalty, and value into your brand.

TEST EVERYTHING AND BE OPEN TO EXPERIMENTATION - OTHERWISE, YOU'RE JUST RUNNING AROUND IN THE DARK.

We all love to have the perfect marketing plan in place, but the reality is that you won't know what works and what doesn't until you start testing. And you must be open to experimentation.

The best marketing comes from testing and learning more about your customers. This is especially true for startups.

You can't limit yourself to one marketing channel or strategy. You need to test multiple channels and strategies at once. Don't be afraid of making mistakes - just learn from them:

When it comes to marketing, your best bet is to try, test, and learn as much as possible. That means running a lot of small experiments on a limited budget. If you do this right, each experiment will teach you something. You'll learn from the wins and the losses. But you have to be open to mistakes and failure because that's how you know.

You can't make a work of art by sitting at your desk and drawing or writing for hours on end. You have to get out there and experiment with as many mediums as possible. You need to test different approaches, mediums, and strategies. Take one thing at a time, but don't limit yourself to just one thing either.

What works for one company may not work for another, so you have to find your own way. The only way to do this is by being open to experimentation, and error-prone experiments are okay as long as you learn from them.

HAVE FUN!

It doesn't matter if you're a marketer, a CEO, or an office manager - when you are having fun, you do your best work. I've seen this theory in action time after time, so I'm going to leave it at that.

As marketers, we have a lot to learn from the entertainment industry. They have been doing this stuff for decades and have learned a thing or two about capturing and keeping customers. It's not just about writing a few clever lines and putting together some pretty pictures. When it comes to marketing, the entertainment industry is on another level, and they know how to get people involved with your brand.

So if you're a marketer, take a good look at the entertainment industry. Study their methods and incorporate those into your own marketing strategy.

AND MOST IMPORTANTLY - STRATEGIZE

You don't need to be a genius to be a good marketer. All you need is an intelligent strategy and the willingness to test it out. After that, there's no reason why you can't run your business like a well-oiled machine.

The key is not to think like an amateur, but instead, think like an expert with years of experience. This will help you create the best strategy for your business. And once you have the strategy in place, you'll have everything you need to get results:

Your marketing strategy is the foundation for good marketing - without it, you could spend weeks without any real progress. That's why it's essential to strategize properly before jumping into anything else.

Strategizing is the best way to get a handle on your marketing efforts. It gives you some direction, and it helps you make decisions where you wouldn't have been able to make them before.

The most successful companies strategize. They don't just do things willy-nilly and hope for the best. Instead, they have a plan, and they know exactly what they need to do. And when they don't have a strategy, they create one.

Marketing is not something that is restricted to big companies with much money to throw around. If you can learn from the best, you'll be competitive with the big players in the field - even if you're just starting out.

6

DEVELOPING & APPLYING YOUR STRATEGY

In the world of marketing, strategy drives results. Without a strategy, you have little more than an aim or wish. And wishes don't pay the bills. But a strategy can also be like a weapon in the hands of someone with no idea how to use it. It can be an ineffective, dangerous instrument that causes more harm than good.

For this reason, strategy is not a skill to be taken lightly. It's not free. Learning how to develop and apply a winning strategy is complicated. It's not something you can rush through or do on the cheap. You need to invest time and money in this critical area to get the results you want. Fortunately, it's also one of the most rewarding parts of the whole marketing process.

This chapter will walk you through the seven steps that will help you develop and apply a winning strategy. But, before that, let's learn why this is so important and then create the right strategy for your business.

DEVELOPING YOUR OWN MARKETING STRATEGY (AND STICKING TO IT - AT LEAST LONG ENOUGH TO DERIVE USABLE DATA) IS THE MOST IMPORTANT THING YOU DO FOR ANY BUSINESS.

Many people, including some marketing pros, believe that you have won half the battle if you have a well-designed business card and a great logo.

They also think that what it takes to be successful in business is some creative imagination and the ability to connect with people instantly. While there is some truth to both of those statements, they aren't enough.

Your strategy will determine how you spend your time and money, and whether or not you'll be successful in business. In fact, if you want to succeed as an entrepreneur, your ability to develop a good strategy is more important than anything else.

You understand your business and your customers better than anyone else. You know what you want to accomplish, and that's why you're in business. So why would you spend money on advertising that doesn't support those goals? It makes no sense to waste money on marketing.

I see it all the time: people spend thousands of dollars on advertising every year, yet they are not achieving the results they want. They may not be making any sales at all.

You already understand this but let me give you a more specific example: Suppose you have a small retail store where people can come in and buy your products. If you start advertising by handing out fliers on the street, what is the cost per sale? It's $0! This is free advertising.

Also, you know the kind of people who come into your store. They are the kind of people who respond to a flier on the street corner. These are your target customers, because they have a similar profile in terms of income, and they live in the neighborhood where you have set up shop.

It's not hard to figure out that spending $5,000 on flyers or brochures advertising in a neighborhood where you know exactly how much each sale will cost you is much more effective than spending $10,000 on an ad in The Wall Street Journal (a national magazine) with no idea who is going to read it or whether it will generate any sales. That's just good business sense.

Therefore, you should focus your advertising budget on those marketing activities that will generate the most sales for the least amount of money.

This is a straightforward concept with a powerful impact. It's just common sense. I know you know this too, but I'm going to tell you anyway:

Your strategy determines your success or failure in business.

I'll say that again, because it's important:

Your strategy determines your success or failure in business.

The most successful businesses in the world are not necessarily making the most money. But, they are making the best use of their marketing dollars to achieve their goals. This is because they know how to spend money and time effectively, and they are getting great results.

The key to marketing success is developing a good strategy that gives you control over your marketing dollars and ensures that you spend your marketing dollars on those activities to provide you with the best return on investment (ROI).

YOUR STRATEGY WILL BE UNIQUE TO YOU AND YOUR BUSINESS.

Like all good things, a strategy is a unique and personal thing. Not one strategy fits all businesses.

Even if you are going after the same customers with the same product or service, you will have to develop a strategy that works specifically for your business. Why? Because your customers will be different, and your competition may be different.

It's easy to see why this is important: If you are like most entrepreneurs, you already have a good idea about what it takes to succeed in your particular business. This means that you should be able to create a strategy that captures your strengths and focuses on the things that work for the kind of customers you are trying to attract.

I can't tell you what makes the best strategy for your business. That's something you have to figure out for yourself. But I can give you the tools to make it happen.

UNDERSTAND THE DIFFERENT METHODOLOGIES OF MARKETING BEFORE GETTING INTO BUILDING YOUR OWN STRATEGY

There are three main types of marketing:

1. Product-driven or product-focused: Companies that focus on products.
2. Customer-driven: Companies that focus on customers.
3. Marketing-driven: Companies that focus on marketing.

Most companies combine all three methods, but the most successful ones use a combination of product and customer-driven marketing while using marketing as the driving force behind everything they do.

Why? Because success is directly connected to how well you make your customers feel about doing business with you. The best way to do this is by providing great value for money and being responsive and easy to deal with, both regarding your offer's products and services and how you conduct your business.

Understanding all three marketing methodologies is essential because you will need to combine all three of these approaches in your own strategy. It all depends on the kind of business you are in and the way you do business.

The correct marketing mix will depend on your specific business:

I mentioned the three main types of marketing, but there is a fourth type that is equally important: The marketing mix. The perfect combination of product, place, price, and promotion is called the "marketing mix."

If you are developing a winning strategy, it's critical that you understand the seven steps in the blueprint to create your own marketing strategy.

Step 1 - SWOT analysis

Summary: SWOT analysis (Strengths, Weaknesses, Opportunities, and Threats) is a powerful research tool that helps you to identify your strengths and weaknesses in the marketplace as well as your opportunities and threats. It also allows you to identify the key factors that will affect your success or failure in the market, in addition to the best way to approach them.

Strengths: This is the area where we want to be better than our competitors. It's also the area where our customers are most likely already aware of what we offer.

Weaknesses: This is likely an area where we are weaker than our competitors, and it is usually a place where our customers are not aware that we offer services or products to help them.

Opportunities: This is where you see changes happening in your market that could create business for you if you act quickly enough to take advantage of them before your competitors.

Threats: This is where you see changes happening in your market that could take away business from you if you don't act quickly to prevent them from happening.

For example, if you were a contractor trying to market your services to property owners, you might do a SWOT analysis as follows:

Strengths: Contractors have the necessary skill and experience to provide many of the services property owners need.

Weaknesses: Contractors are often perceived as high-pressure salespeople who end up overcharging for their services.

Opportunities: People are more aware of the importance of good home maintenance and upkeep, so more homeowners are willing to consider hiring contractors.

Threats: Property owners have a growing awareness that some contractors take advantage of them by performing shoddy work at high prices, so they're less likely to hire a contractor.

Step 2: Determine your value proposition.

Your value proposition is the most important marketing message that you will ever develop. It is the one thing that you have to communicate clearly to your customers for them to understand why they should do business with you.

Your value proposition should be easy for your customer to understand, and it should be communicated in a way that immediately connects with them. This can include an expression of how your products and services will affect their lives, how much money they will save, or how much money they can make using your products and services. The idea is to immediately connect with them in terms of what matters most to them.

For example, if you offer products to help people lose weight, your value proposition may be something like this: "Use our products and services to get started on your journey to a healthier life. We have the top-quality products that will help you reach your goals faster than you ever thought possible."

Another example could be: "We can help you to make your business profitable finally, and that's what you really want. Our business solutions program will help you to make your business profitable finally, and that's what you really want."

Step 3 - what are your marketing strategy objectives?

Your marketing messages represent exactly what you are going to tell people so that they will be able to understand why it is essential for them to do business with you. The more clearly you understand your marketing messages, the easier it will be for you to develop the specific tactics you will use to help your customers see the value of doing business.

The primary objective of all of your marketing messages should be to immediately connect with your customers in a way that makes them want to do business with you. Your secondary objective should be to make it easy for people who want to do business with you to do so, whether they buy from you online or from a brick and mortar store.

For example, if you have a brick-and-mortar store, your marketing messages should be read by people who come into your store to understand what you have to offer quickly. In addition, your marketing messages should help them easily find the products or services that they are looking for them to do business with you.

If you are an online seller, your marketing messages should be designed to tell customers everything they need to know about how you can help them make their lives better, whether they are looking for ways to improve their health or improve their financial situation. In addition, your marketing messages should be easy for people who want to do business with you to find and buy from you online.

Step 4: Make sure you understand your customer.

This is one of the most critical steps you take. First, you must understand your customer, what they want and how they want it. Once you have this information, you'll be able to create a marketing strategy that will help you reach your customer. You need to know the following:

What are their needs?

How does your company meet its needs?

For example, if you owned an electric company, your customers would be the people who need electricity. But what do they need? They need to heat and cool their home. You can meet that need by providing a reliable source of electricity to heat and cool their homes.

Another example, if you owned a coffee shop, you would be marketing to people who want a good cup of coffee. Your marketing will be directed toward those who drink coffee, but what they want is a good cup of Joe. You can meet their needs by providing them with high-quality coffee and the atmosphere that goes with it.

Step 5 - Define your Avatars

Your avatar is the "ideal customer" that you're trying to attract. You can think about your avatar as someone looking for the services or products you offer and that your business can provide. To define your avatar, do the following:

Define – What makes up the ideal customer? Age, gender, income, marital status, education level, job type?

Determine – How many of these people are there in your market?

Develop – Create a profile for each of these people. Think about what they like and don't like. What kind of things would they be interested in? What kind of things do they hate? What types of things would they want different from what they have now?

For example, if you owned a business that sold nutritional supplements, your avatar might be a 30-something male who works out regularly at the gym. Here's how you can create a profile:

Age: 30-something

Gender: male

Income: $55,000 to $75,000 per year (educated guess)

Marital status: single or married with no children (educated guess)

Education Level: some college or trade school training (an educated guess based on the income level)

Job Type: works in an office or the healthcare field (educated guess based on the income level and education level) This type of person might be interested in a supplement that will increase his energy level and endurance at the gym. But he would want a product that tastes good enough that he's willing to take it regularly. He might also want a product that doesn't have a harmful side effects, like being jittery or shaky.

Step 6: Study and research the market and your competitors.

In this step, you will learn how to use market research to your advantage. Market research can help you understand the target market, the ideal customer, and the competition. This research will also help you to develop your marketing plan.

Here are the key questions to answer:

Who is my target market?

What can I do to attract them? (i.e., what's my offer?)

What makes my products/services different from those of my competitors? (i.e., value proposition)

How much is each of my products/services worth to different customers? (i.e., how much value will they add?)

How much profit do I need to earn per sale? (i.e., what is my pricing strategy?)

What is the competition doing, and how can I use that information to my advantage?

Here's an example of how you can use market research to answer these questions:

Who is my target market?

You are targeting the 30-something male who works out regularly at the gym.

What can I do to attract them? (i.e., what's my offer?) First, you want to give them something they can't get from your competitors. You have a product that tastes good and has no side effects. This is a product that will increase their energy level and endurance at the gym. But they will also like the fact that it doesn't cost very much. This product doesn't have anything wrong with it, so they don't have to worry about taking too much of it and ending up being sick.

What makes my products/services different from those of my competitors? (i.e., value proposition) Your product tastes good and has no side effects. Your product doesn't cost very much. This product doesn't have anything bad in it, so they don't have to worry about taking too much of it and ending up being sick.

How much is each of my products/services worth to different customers? (i.e., how much value will they add?) $5 per week for a 6-month supply of the supplement (6 x $0.50 = $3 per week or $4 per month) + you get a free workout DVD with your first order = $4.00 per month.

How much profit do I need to earn per sale? (i.e., what is my pricing strategy?) You will sell this product for **$20 per bottle**. There are 30 servings in each bottle, so you need to sell three bottles per month. Your profit margin is $20 - $4 = $16 per sale. This is a 40% profit margin, and you will need to sell three bottles per month at that price point to earn a living off of your business.

What is the competition doing, and how can I use that information to my advantage? Your competition is selling the same product at a higher price point than you are, but they don't have your guarantee. They are selling a supplement that tastes really bad, so their customers have a tough time taking it. They are also selling a supplement with side effects and can make the user feel shaky and jittery.

Step 7 - Establish your best marketing method (based on your target audience)

Your brand is your reputation in the business. It is what people think about you and will be the first thing they notice about your business. It is your commitment to excellence, and it will be the cornerstone of your business.

Here are the key questions to answer:

What is my brand? What will customers associate with me? How do I want my customers to feel about my business? What does my brand say about me? What makes me different from my competition? Finally, how can I use this information to face my business and develop a strategic plan of action? (i.e., how can I create a unique identity and image for my business?)

Here's an example of how you can use this information to develop your branding strategy:

What is my brand? My brand is all about quality and customer service. I want people to think of me as a quality provider. I want them to feel that they will get excellent service and value for their money when they deal with my business.

What will customers associate with me? My customers will associate my brand with quality and customer service. They will also think that I have a positive attitude, am enthusiastic about the products or services that I sell, and care about them as people.

How do I want my customers to feel about my business? My customers should feel good and confident about dealing with me and spending their money on my products/services. My customers should feel like they are doing something good for themselves when they buy from me and like they are getting value for their money.

What does my brand say about me? My brand says that I am a quality provider. It says that I have a positive attitude, am enthusiastic about the products or services that I sell, and care about my customers.

What makes me different from my competition? My competitors are all quality providers, but they don't offer the same guarantee as I do. They don't have the same enthusiasm for their products/services or feel the same level of customer service commitment as I do.

How can I use this information to put a face on my business and develop a strategic plan of action? (i.e., how can I create a unique identity and image for my business?) To put a face on my business, I will use an image that makes my customers feel good about doing business with me. For example, I will use a picture of me smiling in front of the product that I sell with a confident look on my face. I will also be wearing a button-down shirt, dress pants, and nice shoes in this picture. Underneath the image, I will put my slogan: Quality Product + Great Customer Service = You're In Good Hands with Me!

NOW YOU KNOW YOUR BLIND SPOTS!

Now that you are familiar with the steps to developing a marketing strategy, you can create a plan that will work for you. We have covered all the powerful tips and techniques for your success from the experts themselves. In addition, you have learned about a large handful of effective strategies. You should now be able to create a marketing plan that will put you on the fast track to success.

Remember: Design a Marketing Strategy that works for **you**!

CONCLUSION

We've covered much ground in the past 100 reasons, and I hope you've enjoyed reading them as much as I've enjoyed writing them.

As the saying goes, "The more you know, the less you fear" And hopefully, I've given you some things to think about.

In summary, we have learned the following:

The market is a two-way street, and you can't just "sell" to it.

Your success depends on the success of others.

You have to go where the people are, and you have to communicate with them in a language that they understand.

You can't just sell your product. You have to sell yourself, your company, and the whole concept of your product.

You have to give people a REASON TO BUY.

You have to have a REASON TO BELIEVE.

And... You have to be consistent. If you are inconsistent, then you will fail.

Now that you have read my book and shared my knowledge, I wish you all the best of luck with your marketing efforts.

Don't forget to bookmark this page, so that you can quickly come back and re-read any of the 100 reasons (in fact - it would be a good idea to print it out to make notes on each point.)

And if you enjoyed reading this book, then please let me know by sending me an email and leaving a review of the book on Amazon.

I want to thank you for reading my book, and I hope you have found it helpful.

REFERENCES / RESOURCES

https://coschedule.com/blog/how-to-find-your-target-audience

https://blog.hubspot.com/marketing/traditional-marketing-vs-digital-marketing

https://blog.hootsuite.com/reach-vs-impressions/

https://www.hubspot.com/marketing-statistics

https://www.investopedia.com/terms/m/marketing.asp

https://marketinginsidergroup.com/strategy/what-is-marketing/

https://blog.hubspot.com/marketing/what-is-marketing

https://www.analytico.ca/three-purposes-marketing/

https://www.thebalancesmb.com/what-is-marketing-2296057

https://www.yodiz.com/blog/8-types-of-marketing-strategies-and-definition/

https://www.weidert.com/blog/top-10-most-effective-marketing-strategies

https://www.businessknowhow.com/marketing/marketing-plan.htm

https://smallbusiness.chron.com/four-essential-components-marketing-plan-63606.html

https://emarsys.com/learn/blog/4-ps-of-marketing-importance/

https://www.investopedia.com/terms/f/four-ps.asp

https://www.campaignmonitor.com/resources/knowledge-base/what-are-the-4-ps-of-marketing/

https://southmetrics.com/why-marketing-is-not-just-selling/

https://www.bartleby.com/essay/Marketing-Is-Not-Just-Selling-And-Advertising-PKUMRVW5U385

https://toddbrown.me/marketing-not-selling/

https://blog.hurree.co/blog/marketing-mix-7ps

https://www.livescience.com/2431-humans-bother-emotions.html

https://www.psychologytoday.com/us/blog/the-literary-mind/200911/why-do-we-have-emotions

https://www.forbes.com/sites/forbescoachescouncil/2018/05/09/how-your-emotions-influence-your-decisions/?sh=1ca9d54a3fda

https://www.theatlantic.com/science/archive/2016/09/the-best-headspace-for-making-decisions/500423/

https://start.askwonder.com/insights/want-add-previous-request-made-few-years-ago-want-studies-support-idea-decisions-c22yygpap

https://www.mycustomer.com/marketing/strategy/how-research-proves-emotion-is-more-powerful-than-logic-in-marketing

https://www.thedrum.com/news/2019/01/30/why-emotion-plays-critical-role-decision-making

https://www.sciencedirect.com/science/article/pii/S1532046406000451

https://www.bachremedies.com/en-us/explore/blog/2018/how-do-our-emotions-affect-decision-making/

https://cxl.com/blog/online-manipulation-all-the-ways-youre-currently-being-deceived/

https://commitagency.com/blog/emotional-branding-more-than-manipulation/

https://www.cbc.ca/news/business/online-holiday-marketing-1.3355669

https://www.psychologytoday.com/us/blog/inside-the-consumer-mind/201302/how-emotions-influence-what-we-buy

https://fabrikbrands.com/the-power-of-emotional-marketing/

http://www.uriel.org/brand-management/the-origin-of-the-marketing-concept/

https://en.wikipedia.org/wiki/History_of_marketing

https://en.wikipedia.org/wiki/Marketing_strategy

https://www.transifex.com/blog/2016/a-brief-look-at-marketing-through-the-ages/

https://historycooperative.org/the-evolution-of-marketing-from-trade-to-tech/

https://squareup.com/us/en/townsquare/history-of-marketing

https://blog.oxfordcollegeofmarketing.com/2012/11/23/the-6-main-stages-in-marketings-history/

https://en.wikipedia.org/wiki/WLS_(AM)

https://www.allbusiness.com/10-common-marketing-mistakes-to-avoid-3-96534-1.html

REFERENCES / RESOURCES | 163

https://www.benchmarkone.com/blog/8-common-small-business-marketing-mistakes/

https://www.sotrender.com/blog/2020/06/biggest-mistakes-marketers-make/

https://sites.google.com/view/multiple-income-2021/home

https://www.marketo.com/webinars/8-biggest-mistakes-digital-marketers-make-and-how-to-avoid-them/

https://www.forbes.com/sites/forbesbusinesscouncil/2020/01/17/15-common-marketing-mistakes-entrepreneurs-should-avoid/?sh=51ff0e554f87

https://shape.io/stop-ppc-overspending

https://vladimirjones.com/how-to-avoid-campaign-overspend-with-an-automated-budget-monitor/

https://fiveechelon.com/determining-the-right-timing-for-a-product-launch/

https://startingandsustaining.com/chapters/integrations/

https://headchannel.co.uk/6-steps-of-system-integration-process-321

https://www.advertisingweek360.com/right-creative-wrong-audience-whos-really-seeing-your-ads/

https://mann-co.com/5-signs-your-marketing-is-targeting-the-wrong-audience/#:~:text=If%20you%27ve%20been%20getting,you%27ve%20got%20a%20problem.%5C

https://ispeaksocial.com/targeting-wrong-audience/

https://www.marypomerantzadvertising.com/blog

https://womenbelong.com/7-reasons-why-marketing-strategy-is-important-for-your-business/

https://www.lyfemarketing.com/blog/importance-of-a-marketing-strategy/

https://www.forbes.com/sites/larrymyler/2015/08/22/your-strategy-should-be-as-unique-as-your-business/?sh=1706fb37736b

www.ingramcontent.com/pod-product-compliance
Lightning Source LLC
Chambersburg PA
CBHW031625210526
45464CB00004B/1753